Contents

Mrs. Filberts

What's in a name? Behind the "Mrs. Filberts" name stands 77 years of tradition. Mr. and Mrs. Filbert began in 1900, developed and patented shortening and marga- rines. In 1917, Martha Filbert took over the business. Production and marketing operations expanded to serve 5 states around Maryland. "Mrs. Filberts" became a brand name for the newly developed all-vegetable margarine in 1936. Although Martha Filbert died in 1954, "Mrs. Filberts" lives on in various forms. The family business kept up with changing consumer tastes and markets a whipped margarine, corn-oil margarine, diet imitation margarine and Spread 25. Mrs. Filbert knew what her contemporaries wanted. Today, "Mrs. Filberts" carries on the tradition. For goodness sakes, Mrs. Filberts.

Appetizers

Appetizers are the fun food of the world. All people have a word for appetizers. A smiling word.

To a Frenchman it's not luncheon without an *hors d'oeuvre* first course and vermouth in his glass. Italians don't call it dinner without an antipasto first course. The Greek word is *mezes* and a favorite is *hummus* — chick pea salad.

Even in China, hard workers take time for *deem sum* snacks. Translated, *deem sum* is "touch the heart" and a favorite is *quotie'* (pronounced gwah-tie), moreoften called potstickers, for that's what they do unless you grease the pan!

In Spain it's a light dry sherry and *tapas,* but in Cyprus or Lebanon, if you order *mexes* it's a meal — sometimes as many as thirty little dishes.

Here in America we may serve one, two or — at the most — three bite-size appetizers before dinner. Or we can plan to make an evening of it, with a tableful of tempters — an appetizer supper of snacks gathered round the world.

HORS D'OEUVRE VARIES OF FRANCE

Denise Schorr, a teacher of French cooking in Natick and Concord, Massachusetts, says, "A favorite first course for luncheon in France is marinated fresh vegetables, an appetizer we call hors d'oeuvre varies."

Paris-bred Mrs. Schorr teaches her students to spread peeled cucumber slices in layers, sprinkle with salt and refrigerate overnight. The next day these are rinsed with cold water and wrung dry in a towel. The now limp cucumber slices are marinated overnight in two tablespoons each of wine vinegar and oil with a dusting of tarragon — "flavors that complement each other." French cucumbers are served on chilled plates with plenty of crusty bread.

Large beets, nearly the size of oranges, she bakes in the skin, the same as potatoes, for one hour or longer. "These are sweet as honey," Mrs. Schorr says. Sliced cold she serves them with garden-ripe tomatoes, white onion slices, lots of chopped parsley and vinaigrette dressing.

Tiny, sweet carrots she grates to make four cupfuls and marinates with seven tablespoons oil, two tablespoons wine vinegar, one tablespoon lemon juice, some freshly grated black pepper and salt.

Everything except the tomato slices may be stored a day or two in the refrigerator. Serve on chilled plates with crusty bread and glasses of chilled white wine.

CRUDITÉS

French — meaning raw, or crude. An assortment of tender young vegetables presented as a crisp and delicious appetizer. A salute to the home gardener, or the knowledgeable shopper of fresh produce.

Make a handsome bouquet in a bowl or basket of those vegetables in season, interspersed with any of the following: cherry tomatoes, whole scallions and radishes, baby carrots, strips of green and red peppers, of cucumbers and zucchini, hearts of celery, tiny pieces of cauliflower and broccoli, tiny snaps beans, snow peas in the pod, and tiny tight tips of asparagus. For dipping have ready a bowl of your own mayonnaise, made in seconds in the blender, and a simmering pot of bagna cauda (Italian for hot bath sauce) with the salt and tang of anchovies.

BAGNA CAUDA

1 cup (2 sticks) margarine
¼ cup olive oil
4 cloves garlic, minced

6 anchovy fillets, chopped
⅛ teaspoon salt

Heat margarine, olive oil and garlic over low heat until margarine is melted. Add chopped anchovies and salt to keep warm — not too hot — 20 minutes for flavors to blend. Serve as a dip for raw vegetables. Makes 1½ cups.

BLENDER MAYONNAISE

1 egg
2 teaspoons each sugar and paprika
2 teaspoons Dijon-type mustard

3 tablespoons wine vinegar
1 cup salad oil

In blender place egg, sugar, paprika, mustard and vinegar. Blend a few seconds, and with the motor running, gradually pour in salad oil, blending until smooth. Chill. Makes 1½ cups.

Flavor variations:

Before serving mayonnaise stir in lemon juice and a bit of the yellow peel to taste. Or a few drops of hot pepper sauce.

CUCUMBERS IN SOUR CREAM

4 large cucumbers
1 cup sour cream
1 teaspoon salt

¾ teaspoon freshly ground
    black pepper
1 tablespoon grated horseradish

Peel and thinly slice cucumbers. Combine sour cream, salt, pepper and horseradish. Stir together then pour over cucumbers and lightly toss. Chill until ready to serve. 8 servings.

PICKLED BEETS

Slice cold boiled or canned beets to fill one pint jar; add 1 teaspoon horseradish and cider vinegar to cover. Sliced onions may be added. Let stand overnight for flavors to blend.

ITALIAN ANTIPASTO

6 thin slices cooked
  sausage, sweet or hot
6 thin slices salami
6 anchovy fillets
3 celery hearts, halved
  lengthwise
1 (2 ounce) can Italian antipasto,
  optional

1 (4 ounce) can Italian tuna fish
12 large green olives
1 (4 ounce) can pimientos
3 teaspoons capers
6 slices tomato
4 sweet or hot peppers, in oil
  or vinegar

On an attractive serving platter, arrange Italian antipasto and tuna in center and add remaining ingredients for an attractive presentation. Pass oil and vinegar dressing (vinaigrette) or spoon over top. Serve with crusty Italian bread. 6 servings.

VINAIGRETTE DRESSING
(BASIC FRENCH DRESSING)

½ teaspoon each salt, freshly
  ground black pepper
1 teaspoon dry mustard, or Dijon-type

⅓ cup red wine vinegar
1 cup salad oil

In covered jar, shake together dry ingredients then add oil and shake vigorously. Store at room temperature. Shake before using. Makes 1⅓ cups.

Mideastern salad mixture of cracked wheat, mint etc., is spooned onto plate or scooped up in lettuce leaves or pieces of pita bread.

TABBOULEH (OR TABOOLI)

½ cup cracked wheat
2 cups water
2 cups chopped parsley
½ cup chopped mint
1 cucumber, peeled and diced

2 tomatoes, diced
4 scallions, chopped
⅓ cup lemon juice
⅓ cup salad oil
½ teaspoon salt

Soak wheat in water 15 minutes; drain, then use hands to press out moisture. Toss wheat, parsley, mint, cucumber, tomatoes and scallions together. Add lemon juice, oil and salt and toss to blend. Serve cold in a bowl. Pass lettuce or romaine leaves or pita bread for scooping up. 10 servings.

Greek and Mideastern chick pea salad to eat with a fork, or scoop up with pita bread or crackers.

HUMMUS BI TAHINI

½ cup tahini, purchased in
   Mideastern store
½ cup water
¼ cup salad oil
¼ cup lemon juice
4 garlic cloves, peeled

2 cans garbanzos (chick peas),
   drained
6 scallions, chopped
salt, pepper
¼ cup chopped parsley

Into blender put tahini, water, salad oil, lemon juice and garlic. Blend until smooth. Add chick peas and blend thoroughly. Stir in chopped scallions, salt and pepper to taste. Serve in two flat soup plates with parsley sprinkled on top. 12 servings.

Guotie (pronounced gwah-tie) is the Chinese name for these shrimp filled dumplings you pan brown, steam cook and serve hot with chili dipping sauce. Plan on four apiece!

POTSTICKERS — FROM CHINA

3 cups unsifted flour
½ teaspoon salt
1 cup water
margarine

shrimp filling (see recipe)
1 cup beef consommé
chili dipping sauce (see recipe)

Mix flour and salt with fork then gradually add water, stirring to make dough. Turn onto floured board and knead until smooth, 5 minutes. Cover with a damp cloth and let rest 30 minutes.

Divide dough into 2 equal balls. Roll one portion ⅛ inch thick then cut into circles with 3-inch cutter or can top. Place 2 teaspoons shrimp filling in each cirlce and fold dough to make half-circle. Press edges together to seal. Set potsticker on plate seam side up, so dumpling sits flat. As you work, keep covered to prevent drying out. (May freeze at this stage.)

To cook, brush 12-inch skillet generously with margarine and arrange potstickers seam-side-up without touching. Cook over moderate heat until bottoms are golden brown. Pour ¼ cup beef consommé into pan, cover tightly and let steam over low heat 10 minutes (15 minutes for frozen). Use spatula to remove potstickers — brown side up — onto heated serving plates. Serve hot with small cups of chili sauce for dipping. Makes 4 dozen — 12 servings.

Shrimp Filling

½ pound cooked shrimp, in shells
½ pound ground pork or beef
1 cup very finely shredded cabbage
¼ cup minced scallion

½ cup chopped mushrooms
1 clove garlic, minced
¼ teaspoon salt
2 tablespoons soy sauce

Shell and chop shrimp; mix well with remaining ingredients. Makes about 2½ cups.

Chili Dipping Sauce

½ cup soy sauce
½ cup beef consommé
¼ cup sesame or salad oil

2 tablespoons vinegar
1 teaspoon hot pepper sauce

Blend all ingredients and serve in individual dipping cups to accompany potstickers. Makes 1⅓ cups.

CHINESE BARBECUED PORK

2 pounds pork butt
1 clove garlic, minced
1 teaspoon salt
½ teaspoon ground ginger
1 tablespoon sugar

2 tablespoons sherry
3 tablespoons soy sauce
2 tablespoons honey
½ teaspoon Chinese "five spice"
  (in jars)

Cut pork butt into strips ½ inch by ½ inch. Put into plastic bag with remaining ingredients and place on larger plate. Marinate 1 hour, turning occasionally to blend. Remove meat from marinade to shallow baking pan and roast in 325°F. oven 1½ hours, basting frequently with marinade and drippings. 10 appetizer servings.

CRUSHED TOASTED SESAME SEED

To be sprinkled on salad, barbecued meat or pieces of crusty bread for interesting flavor and texture. Place a single layer of seed in a heavy skillet over moderate heat; stir and cook until golden brown. Pour seed into blender with 1 teaspoon salt for each cup of seed. Blend to crush seeds. Store in a tightly covered jar.

SKEWERED SHRIMP

1 pound frozen raw, shelled shrimp
2 green peppers, seeded
8 slices bacon, cut in sixths
3 (4-ounce) cans button mushrooms,
  drained

½ cup (1 stick) margarine
1 teaspoon salt
dash of hot pepper sauce

Thaw shrimp. Rinse with cold water. Cut green peppers in 1-inch squares. Alternate shrimp, peppers, bacon and mushrooms on 48 skewers or round toothpicks, about 3-inches long. Place kabobs on a well greased broiler pan. Melt margarine with salt, hot pepper sauce and use to brush kabobs. Place 4-inches under broiler and broil 5 minutes; turn kabobs and broil another 5 minutes, basting once. Makes 48 kabobs.

Tiny turnovers in cheese pastry can be made ahead, refrigerated or frozen to bake in 15 minutes.

SALMON BITES

---

1 (16-ounce) can salmon	1 teaspoon grated horseradish
4 slices bacon	1 teaspoon minced onion
¾ cup condensed Cheddar cheese soup	dash hot pepper sauce
	Cheese Canapé pastry

Drain and flake salmon (crush bones — they're rich in calcium). Fry bacon until crisp; crumble. Combine all ingredients except pastry. Chill.

Cheese Canapé Pastry

1 cup (2 sticks) margarine	2 cups flour
1 cup shredded Cheddar cheese	dash salt, pepper

Cream margarine and cheese. Add flour and seasonings. Mix thoroughly. Shape dough into a ball. Chill at least 3 hours. To assemble, roll pastry very thin and cut in 2½-inch squares. Place a heaping teaspoonful of the salmon on half of each square. Fold over and press edges with a fork. Place turnovers on cookie sheets. Bake 10 minutes in 450°F. oven; a little longer when chilled and frozen. Makes 80 appetizers.

CHEESE POT PRONTO

Grate and combine pieces of cheese with an equal amount of margarine. Whip smooth with a little sherry or brandy. Refrigerate in an attractive pot and serve in the same. For flavor and ease of spreading, serve at room temperature.

NOVA SCOTIA NIBBLES

16 frozen fried fish sticks
½ cup grated Parmesan cheese

2 tablespoons margarine
Sea Sauce

Cut fish sticks in thirds. Roll each cut in cheese. Melt margarine in shallow baking pan, 15 by 10-inches. Place fish in pan. Bake in very hot oven, 450 degrees for 8 to 10 minutes. Turn carefully. Bake another 8 to 10 minutes, until crisp and brown. Serve hot with Sea Sauce. Makes 48 nibbles.

Sea Sauce

1 (8-ounce) can tomato sauce
¼ cup chili sauce or catsup
¼ teaspoon each garlic powder
    and oregano

dash of hot pepper sauce
dash of sugar, of basil

Combine all ingredients. Simmer 10 minutes, stirring occasionally. Makes 1 cup sauce.

Delectable appetizer and quick to do as guests watch. It's from the nation's Dairy State, where one community is called Holland for the great Gouda and Edam cheese it produces.

WISCONSIN FRIED CHEESE

2 egg whites
1 tablespoon water
8 slices Gouda or Edam cheese,
   cut ½ inch thick

fine dry bread or cracker crumbs
margarine

Beat egg whites and water until frothy. Dip cheese slices into beaten egg whites, then into dry bread crumbs. Let stand 10 minutes. Heat about ½ inch deep margarine in heavy skillet over moderate heat. Quickly fry cheese until golden brown on both sides — takes only minutes. Serve with wine or beer. 8 servings.

Crunchy bread sticks to make ahead of time. Freeze some if you like.

SOUTHLAND SESAME STICKS

¾ cup (1½ sticks) margarine
2 cups unsifted flour
1 teaspoon salt

2 dashes cayenne pepper
¼ cup ice water
1 cup sesame seed

Preheat oven to 325°F. Cut margarine into the flour, salt and pepper. Sprinkle ice water over dough while tossing it with a fork until it forms a ball. Roll out on floured board to ⅛ inch thickness and cut into 1 inch wide sticks. Place on ungreased baking sheets and sprinkle generously with sesame seed. Bake 15 minutes. Before removing from pan and while still hot, sprinkle with a little salt. Makes 3 dozen sticks. These freeze perfectly.

NEW ENGLAND CODFISH CAKES

1 pound salt codfish
4 to 5 medium size potatoes,
    uncooked

1 egg
¼ teaspoon pepper
margarine

Soak fish in cold water to cover overnight. Drain and add peeled, sliced potatoes. Cover with cold water and boil until potatoes are cooked, about 15 minutes. Drain thoroughly in colander and return to saucepan. Mash fish and potatoes together, adding whole egg and pepper. Beat with fork. Using a spoon, scoop up the mixture and shape with fork so the cakes are "whiskery." Slide onto platter until ready to fry. To fry, have ¼ inch hot melted margarine in skillet over moderate heat. Fry crusty gold on each side, turning once. Serve hot. Makes 12 to 24 cakes, depending on size.

Variation:

2 (8 oz) cans Fish Cake Mix
3 tablespoons minced onion
2 eggs

2 tablespoons melted margarine
an olive, cracker triangles and
    paprika for garnish

Preheat oven to 375°F. Mix all ingredients together thoroughly. Brush margarine over a cookie sheet. Turn fish mixture onto sheet. Using your hands and a flexible medium spatula, shape mixture into form of a fish. Brush surface with more margarine. Bake 45 minutes. Remove to serving platter. Garnish with stuffed olive slices for eye, cracker triangles for fins and a sprinkle of paprika for color. Have more fish ready for the oven if you are serving a large crowd. 4 to 6 servings.

QUICK LIVERWURST PATÉ

½ pound favorite liverwurst
2 tablespoons margarine

1 teaspoon salt
hot pepper sauce to taste

Whirr in blender until smooth as silk. Chill. Makes 2 cups of paté.

SHRIMP PATÉ

½ pound cooked, shelled shrimp
or
2 (4½-ounce) cans shrimp, drained
½ cup (1 stick) margarine
2 tablespoons each lemon juice,
   grated horseradish

¼ teaspoon each salt, nutmeg
dash hot pepper sauce
tiny shrimp or chopped parsley
   garnish

Grind shrimp, then cream with margarine. Add seasonings; mix thoroughly. Chill. Remove Shrimp Paté from mold to serving plate. Surround base with tiny shrimp or the chopped parsley or fresh lemon wedges, edged with paprika. Serve with crusty bread, pumpernickel or fresh vegetables from the garden. Makes 1½ cups of spread.

Soups & Stews

From New Orleans to New England, the West Indies to Wyoming, soups and stews have for all times and all places served in an infinite variety of capacities.

They may introduce the meal, or be the main course. They may warm the diner, or be light and cool to the palate; stimulate the appetite, or soothe frazzled nerves. Indeed, healing powers have been attributed to some — notably chicken soup — and just what is a witch's brew?

Whatever the ingredients, soups and stews allow the cook the greatest opportunity to use his or her imagination as well as leftovers. This glossary will help you to know what you've created:

Soup: a liquid made by boiling meat, fish, vegetables and various ingredients.

Stew: a preparation of meat, fish or other food by stewing.

Chowder: U.S. soup or stew with clams, fish or vegetables potatoes and onions and other ingredients.

Gumbo: Stew or thick soup with okra, chicken or seafood — sometimes with filé as thickener.

In the deep South GUMBO is a hearty soup that is highly regarded. Every good chef in the famous New Orleans restaurants closely guards his blend of herbs and spices. The unusual flavoring known as "filé" is made of the tender leaves of the sassafrass tree, finely ground. It is pronounced "fee-lay" and looks somewhat like dill weed in a jar. It usually can be ordered or bought from a specialty grocery store or shop. This recipe uses filé and also uses a turkey carcass with meat on it. Good for Thanksgiving leftovers!

TURKEY GUMBO

Turkey carcass with meat on it
2 tablespoons margarine
¾ lb ham, diced
1 large onion, chopped
2 sprigs parsley, chopped
1 sprig of thyme, chopped

1 bay leaf, crushed
½ hot red pepper, seeded
   and chopped fine
2 tablespoons filé powder
salt to taste
4 cups hot boiled rice

Remove turkey meat from carcass and dice. Melt margarine in large iron or enameled pot, and sauté meat and ham. Add onion, parsley and thyme and cook for 6 minutes, stirring constantly. Add 2½ quarts boiling water, bay leaf, red pepper and the turkey carcass. Simmer for 1½ hours. Remove from heat. Take out turkey carcass and discard. Stir in salt and filé. Serve piping hot with half a cup of cooked rice in each soup plate. If you plan this recipe for more than one meal do not put the filé in the reserved portion until you are ready to serve it. Reheated filé can sometimes become sticky. 8 servings.

PERFECT RICE EVERY TIME

4 cups water
2 teaspoons salt

2 cups long grain rice

Using large saucepan (rice expands three times during cooking) bring salted water to boiling. Stir in rice and cover tightly. Reduce heat to low and simmer rice 20 minutes (use timer). All water will be absorbed and separate grains of rice will be tender. Toss with fork and keep warm — up to 30 minutes — for serving. Extra rice may be refrigerated or frozen for later use. 8 to 10 servings.

Another New Orleans specialty. This is a hearty stew-like soup easily made in your own kitchen.

NEW ORLEANS SHRIMP GUMBO
---

2 lbs shrimp
4 tablespoons margarine
1 tablespoon instant
  minced onion
1½ cup chopped celery
½ green pepper, chopped
1 clove garlic, sliced
4 cups fresh or frozen
  okra, sliced
2 tablespoons flour

4 teaspoons chicken
  seasoned stock base
4 cups water
1 (1 lb, 13 oz.) can tomatoes
½ lb cubed cooked ham
1 bayleaf
1 teaspoon thyme
1 tablespoon gumbo
  filé powder
4 cups hot steamed rice

Cook and clean shrimp; cut into bite size pieces, (Or, us frozen shrimp.) Heat margarine in large kettle or dutch oven. Add onion, celery, green pepper and garlic; sauté lightly. Dredge okra with flour. If you are using frozen okra thaw it first. Add okra to kettle. Continue to sauté for a few minutes. Add seasoned stock base, water, tomatoes, ham, bayleaf and thyme leaves. Lower heat; cover and simmer 1 hour. Add shrimp and cook 15 minutes longer. Remove from heat. Mix 4 or 5 tablespoons of the hot soup with the gumbo filé, then add to soup. Stir off of heat about 5 minutes or until thickened. Do not cook after gumbo filé is added. Serve in soup bowls. In New Orleans a spoonful of hot cooked rice is always placed in the center of each serving. 8 servings.

RICE PILAF
---

2 tablespoons margarine
1 cup finely chopped onion
1 cup rice

2 cups chicken or beef
  broth or tomato juice

Melt margarine in 1½ quart saucepan. Add onion and cook over medium heat until onion is soft, not brown. Add rice and stir until golden — not brown. Add liquid and stir; bring to boil. Cover and reduce heat; simmer 20 minutes, until liquid is absorbed and rice tender. Serve hot. 4 to 5 servings.

The United States Senate Dining Room in Washington, D.C., is famous for this bean soup.

G.I. BEAN SOUP

1½ lbs small navy beans
3 quarts water
2 large onions, coarsely chopped
1 large clove garlic, minced
2 tablespoons margarine
bouquet garni (4 sprigs of
   parsley, 1 large bay leaf,
   1 teaspoon thyme)

1½ lbs ham hocks with meat
  on them (see note)
3 teaspoons black pepper
salt to taste

Soak beans overnight in water to cover (8 hours at least). Next day drain beans, rinse in hot water to whiten. Pour three quarts water into soup kettle, bring to boil. Put margarine in skillet with onions and garlic; cook slowly stirring occasionally until both are slightly brown. Make bouquet garni. When water has come to a boil, add beans, onions and garlic, bouquet garni, ham (hocks or pieces) and pepper. Bring to a boil again, reduce heat, cover and simmer three hours. Remove from heat, discard bouquet garni. Remove ham hocks if you have used them. Strip, and discard bones, skin, fat and gristle. Chop lean meat into small pieces and reserve. Place 1 pint soup into blender, blend 45 seconds at high speed. Return to kettle and stir well. This helps thicken the soup, which should be almost a purée but with bits of ham and whole beans showing. If thicker soup is desired, remove 1 cup soup, stir into it 2 tablespoons arrowroot or flour to make paste. Pour and stir this into soup. Bring soup to boil, taste and adjust seasoning. Salt must not be added until just before serving. 8 servings.

Note: You may use left over ham, diced pork, luncheon meat, or a 1 pound ham slice, cut into small pieces and served with soup. This would replace the ham hocks.

This is a delicate, tasty soup. You may like it well enough to keep a pot of fresh mint growing among your plants.

MINTED CREAM OF PEA SOUP

1 (11 ounce) can condensed green pea soup	2 teaspoons chives, finely chopped
2 soup cans of milk	¼ cup cream
3 tablespoons fresh mint, finely chopped	¼ cup milk
1 teaspoon sugar	sour cream
	mint sprigs

Mix the soup, 2 cans of milk, chopped mint, sugar and chives. Heat to a simmer. Cool. Stir in the ¼ cup cream and ¼ cup milk. Chill. Garnish with spoonfuls of sour cream and tiny mint sprigs. 4 Servings.

An unusually good soup with a delightfully different flavor. You start with a meat stock and vegetables. Then the cider and yogurt enhance the fresh tartness.

SPINACH CIDER SOUP

4 cups meat stock	½ lb spinach, chopped
4 carrots, diced	1 tablespoon minced parsley
1 stalk celery, chopped	1 teaspoon dill weed
3 tablespoons margarine	½ cup apple cider
1 onion chopped	1 cup plain yogurt
½ clove garlic, crushed	4 egg yolks
4 tablespoons flour	salt and pepper to taste

Bring stock to boil in large saucepan. It can be made from bouillon cubes and water. Add carrots and celery; cook until tender. Remove from heat. In a small skillet, melt margarine and saute onion until transparent. Add garlic and flour; stir and cook for 2 minutes. Combine ½ cup soup stock with onion mixture, stirring constantly; add mixture to cooked vegetables. Add spinach, parsley, dill and cider. Season and bring to a boil. Beat yogurt and egg yolks together; pour into soup. Reheat, but do not allow to boil. Serve hot. 6 servings.

Counting calories can be less painful if you manage to slip this delicious summer soup into your menu. It can be on his or her diet list . . . or both.

FROSTY CUCUMBER SOUP

2 cups buttermilk
2 cups yogurt
1½ cups peeled and finely
   chopped cucumbers
1 tablespoon finely chopped
   green onion

2 teaspoons lemon juice
salt and pepper to taste
1 tablespoon chopped fresh
   dill, or, 1 teaspoon dill weed
6 thin lemon slices

Blend together buttermilk and yogurt. Combine mixture with cucumbers, onion, lemon juice, salt, pepper and dill. Chill. Just before serving, mix again and pour into chilled consomme cups, or chilled old-fashioned drink glasses. Garnish with lemon slices. 6 servings.

This extremely good soup could be your first course for a formal dinner, a hearty brunch on a cold holiday, or just plain dinner for two. It is remarkably easy to make.

DELICIOUS CRABMEAT SOUP

1 (11 ounce) can condensed cream
   of celery soup
1 soup can of milk
1 cup flaked crab meat
dash of Worcestershire sauce

pinch of mace
2 to 3 tablespoons sherry
2 hard-cooked eggs
chopped fresh parsley

In a medium saucepan combine soup, milk, crab meat, Worcestershire and mace. Heat. Stir in sherry and add chopped hard-cooked egg whites. Continue cooking for a few minutes more. Sprinkle with sieved hard-cooked egg yolks and chopped parsley. 4 servings.

A hearty main dish soup. Whether it's his or her turn to cook, this chowder and a salad will make the meal.

COLONIAL CHOWDER

⅓ cup chopped onion
⅓ cup chopped celery
3 tablespoons margarine
1 (8 ounce) can minced clams
1 (12 ounce) can whole
   kernel corn

salt and pepper
1 bay leaf
1¼ cups milk
2 tablespoons dry instant potato
2 cups small curd cottage cheese
fresh or dried dill

Cook onion and celery in margarine until soft. Add clams and juice, corn and juice, salt, pepper and bayleaf. Simmer 6 or 8 minutes. Add milk, instant potato, and cottage cheese. Stir thoroughly and bring back to simmer. Taste and correct seasoning. Pour into tureen for table serving, or individual soup bowls. Sprinkle top with chopped fresh dill or dried dill weed. 4 servings.

When you are looking for "something different" here's your soup. Makes a light lunch on hot days. Good for the picnic thermos. Right for a formal party.

CREAM OF LETTUCE SOUP

1 head Boston lettuce
4 scallions, chopped fine
2 tablespoons margarine
½ clove garlic, minced
2 tablespoons chopped parsley
salt and pepper to taste
1 tablespoon almonds, blanched

2 cups chicken broth or bouillon
1 egg yolk
¼ cup heavy cream, heated
¼ cup chopped parsley
3 strips lean bacon, cooked
   and crumbled

Wash and dry the lettuce and separate the leaves. Sauté the scallions in margarine until tender. Add the garlic, parsley, salt, pepper, lettuce leaves and 1 cup water. Cover and simmer for 15 minutes. Add the almonds and purée the mixture in a blender. Add the chicken broth and bring the entire mixture to a boil. Beat the egg yolk with the cream and stir into the soup. Garnish with chopped parsley and crumbled bacon. 4 servings.

An old world recipe worth preserving.

SOUP WITH CHESTNUT CUSTARD

---

1 egg
2 egg yolks
¾ cup heavy cream
⅓ cup thick chestnut purée*
dash of nutmeg

1 teaspoon sugar
dash of salt
1 cup dry white wine
5 cups clear consommé
freshly grated orange peel

*Chestnut purée is available in cans year round. Fresh in season.

Preheat oven to 300°F. Beat egg with egg yolks until light. Stir in cream and chestnut purée. Add nutmeg, sugar and salt. Turn into a shallow greased baking dish. Set in pan of hot water and bake until custard is firm. Cool. Cut the cooled custard into tiny circles, diamonds or other fancy shapes.

Add wine to consommé and heat. Garnish with the custard shapes and sprinkle with grated orange peel. 4 to 6 servings.

From the West Indies comes a marvelous party dish. It can be frozen and defrosted when you want to serve it.

BARBADOS PARTY BEEF STEW

---

3 lbs beef chuck, cut in
   1½ inch cubes
3 tablespoons flour
1 tablespoon margarine
1 lb can tomatoes
2 medium onions, sliced
1 teaspoon celery salt
1 teaspoon salt
¼ teaspoon pepper

⅓ cup vinegar
⅓ cup unsulphured molasses
1 cup water
6 carrots, pared and
   cut in pieces
½ cup raisins
½ teaspoon ginger
4 cups hot boiled rice

Sprinkle beef with the flour. Brown in margarine in heavy saucepan; add tomatoes, onions, celery salt, salt and pepper. Combine vinegar, molasses and water; add to meat. Cover and simmer until meat is tender, about 2 hours. Add carrots, raisins and ginger. Cook until carrots are tender. Serve over hot rice. 12 servings.

Fish

"The Whale that wanders round the Pole
Is not a table fish.
You cannot bake or boil him whole
Nor serve him in a dish." Belloc, *A Bad Child's Book of Beasts*

Maybe not whale, but there is an increasingly great variety of fish available for our enjoyment, and Americans, who used to be behind the rest of the world in eating fish, are fast catching up. You no longer need to live near the seashore to savor the flavor of fresh ocean fish, and it's on the menu all year round.

Like company, fish can be delightful if properly treated, but becomes unpleasant if neglected. So, learn how best to bake, broil or boil — and serve in a dish.

Don't Overcook

- Cooking fish at too high a temperature, or for too long a time toughens them, dries them out, and destroys their fine flavor.
- Fish are cooked when the flesh loses its translucent appearance and becomes opaque.
- Test for doneness — the flesh flakes easily when pierced with a fork. Always place fork in the thickest part of flesh, where it takes the longest to cook.

Know Your Product

- For best results in preparing fish, determine whether it is fat or lean. Both can be cooked by a basic cooking method, but lean fish requires more added fat during cooking to keep them moist and flavorful.
- Fat fish are those containing more than 5 percent fat, such as mackerel, salmon and tuna.
- Lean fish contain less than 5 percent fat. Examples are red snapper, flounder, cod, haddock, and halibut. All shellfish are lean.

Methods of Cooking

Poaching is cooking in simmering liquid.
Steaming is cooking by steam generated from boiling water.
Baking is cooking by dry heat.
Broiling is a dry heat method of cookery. The heat is direct, intense and comes from only one source.
Charcoal Broiling is cooking over hot coals.
Deep fat frying is cooking in a deep layer of fat.
Pan-frying is a method of cooking in a small amount of fat.
Oven-frying produces a product similar to fried fish and does not require turning or basting. Use greased baking pan; pour oil or fat over fish; have oven at 500°F. Good method for large groups. High heat takes only minutes for moist fish with crusty outside.

From India to Britain to the Colonies — many British still eat Kedgeree for breakfast, using the favorite Scotish fish, "Finnan Haddie," which is smoked haddock. If Finnan Haddie is hard to find, try some other fish. This recipe uses canned tuna.

KEDGEREE

2 cups cooked rice (cooked with salt, pepper and ½ teaspoon curry powder)
3 tablespoons chopped parsley
½ cup evaporated milk
2 tablespoons margarine

1 tablespoon lemon juice
3 hard cooked eggs, chopped
2 cups flaked tuna or other flaked, cooked fish
½ cup snipped parsley (garnish only)

Mix all ingredients (except parsley) together lightly and heat thoroughly. Use double boiler on top on range or baking pan placed in pan of water in 350°F oven for about 30 minutes. Can be served hot or cold for breakfast, luncheon or supper. Good with green vegetable or salad. 6 to 8 servings.

A delicate way with a delicate fish. Quick and easy to do. Great choice for health-seeking calorie counters.

SWEET AND SOUR POACHED FISH

1 cup orange juice
1 teaspoon grated orange peel
¼ cup unsulphured molasses
2 tablespoons soy sauce
3 tablespoons lemon juice

½ teaspoon ground ginger
2 pounds flounder fillets
1½ tablespoons cornstarch
lemon slices, small green onions or sliced cucumber for garnish

Combine orange juice, orange peel and ginger. Reserve ¼ of mixture; pour remainder into large skillet. Blend together molasses, soy sauce, lemon juice and ginger. Add to skillet. Bring combined mixtures to boil. Add fillets; reduce heat until mixture is simmering. Cover and cook 10 minutes. Carefully remove fillets to serving platter; keep warm. Prepare sauce by combining cornstarch with reserved orange mixture. Quickly stir this into skillet and cook, stirring constantly until slightly thickened. Garnish fish with lemon slices, small green onions or sliced cucumber. Serve with sauce. 6 servings.

"Will please your heart, your palate and your pocketbook," says Anne, a bright young New Yorker. She leaves her publishing job evenings to become an enthusiastic cook. This is one of her do-it-yourself specials. Very good for long, lazy summer afternoons.

ANNE'S TUNA SPINACH LOAF

1 pound fresh spinach	½ cup freshly grated Parmesan
1½ slices good white bread, crusts	cheese
trimmed	Salt and pepper to taste
½ cup milk	3 tablespoons dry bread crumbs
1 (7-ounce) can tuna in water	4-thickness cheesecloth about
4 anchovy fillets	12″ x 14″ square
2 eggs	Metal bread pan 9 x 5 inches

Rinse spinach, remove stems. With only moisture clinging to leaves put spinach in covered pot over low heat. Cook until spinach is tender, then cool. Soak bread slices in milk about ten minutes, turning once. Remove liquid from spinach by pressing in strainer or by squeezing. Put into mixing bowl and chop fine. Empty tuna and liquid into blender. Add anchovies. Whirr smooth or puree. Add to spinach. Add eggs, cheese, salt, pepper and bread crumbs. Mix thoroughly. Add soaked bread slices (first squeezed dry) and mix again. Scoop mixture onto work counter or cookie sheet and form into loaf approximately 2¾″ wide by 8½″ long. Roll loaf onto cheesecloth, covering completely. Secure ends with twist-tie closures. Put loaf into metal bread pan, cover with water and set over medium heat until boiling. Reduce heat, then simmer about 35 to 45 minutes until done. If you are sure it is firm to touch, it's done. Remove from water. Unroll loaf from cheesecloth onto plate and let cool. Refrigerate overnight. Serve in slices. Garnish with half lemon slice topped with raw carrot slice. You may prefer to brush each slice with olive oil and lemon juice, especially if you have not used Italian Tuna in olive oil. This loaf is long keeping. The older it gets the better it tastes. 30 slices approximately ¼″ thick.

SHRIMP WIGGLE

¾ pound cooked, shelled shrimp	2 cups milk
¼ cup (½ stick) margarine	1 cup cooked peas
¼ cup flour	Patty shells, toast cups,
1 teaspoon salt	or toast

Cut shrimp in half. Melt margarine; blend in flour and salt. Add milk gradually and cook until thick and smooth, stirring constantly. Stir in peas and shrimp; heat. Serve in patty shells, toast cups, or on toast. 6 servings.

An elegant dish for entertaining. Fine for a heating tray on a buffet. Can be prepared ahead and held for baking time.

SOLE SUPREME

4 tablespoons (½ stick) margarine
1 tablespoon flour
½ teaspoon salt
2 teaspoons lemon juice, (divided into ½ teaspoon and 1½ teaspoons)
¼ teaspoon prepared white horseradish
⅛ teaspoon Worcestershire sauce
⅛ teaspoon onion salt
dash of Tabasco sauce

⅓ cup milk
1 (7 ounce) can crabmeat, boned and flaked
4 sole or flounder fillets
2 tablespoons margarine, melted paprika
1 (10 ounce) package frozen lima beans
lemon slices and parsley for garnish

Preheat oven to 350°F. Melt 2 tablespoons margarine in saucepan with flour. Add salt, ½ teaspoon of the lemon juice, horseradish, Worcestershire, onion salt, Tabasco. Blend in milk and cook until thickened, stirring constantly. Remove from heat. Add crabmeat and mix well. Arrange 2 fillets in greased shallow casserole and spread each with half the crab mixture. Top with two remaining fillets. Combine 2 tablespoons margarine, melted with 1½ teaspoon lemon juice and brush over fillets. Sprinkle generously with paprika. Bake for 25 to 30 minutes or until fish flakes easily when tested with fork. Meanwhile, cook lima beans with water according to package directions. To serve, arrange beans around cooked fish. Garnish with lemon slices and parsley. 4 servings. May be doubled or tripled for party serving.

GULF SHRIMP SALAD

1 pound cooked, peeled shrimp
2 cups cooked rice
1 cup sliced celery
½ cup chopped parsley
¼ cup sliced ripe olives

½ cup mayonnaise
2 tablespoons French dressing
2 tablespoons lemon juice
1 teaspoon curry powder
salad greens

Cut shrimp crosswise in half. Combine rice, celery, parsley, olives and shrimp in bowl. In separate bowl, combine mayonnaise, French dressing, lemon juice and curry powder; mix well. Add mayonnaise mixture to shrimp mixture; toss lightly. Chill. Serve on salad greens. 6 servings.

This hearty, tempting, molded salad is welcome on any buffet table. You can make it your specialty. Clever cooks PLAN to have some leftover fish to make it.

TURBOT MOUSSE

1 envelope (1 tablespoon) unflavored
  gelatin
½ cup cold water or fish stock
1 cup mayonnaise or salad dressing
1 cup sour cream
2 cups flaked, poached turbot or
  any other white fish
½ cup diced celery

½ cup diced unpeeled, seeded
  cucumber
3 tablespoons minced onion
4 tablespoons minced stuffed
  green olives
2 tablespoons lemon juice
½ teaspoon each salt and paprika

Soften gelatin in cold water; dissolve over hot water. Stir into mayonnaise. Add sour cream and blend well. Add remaining ingredients and stir until well mixed. Oil a 6-cup decorative mold or individual molds with salad oil. Fill mold, making sure no air pockets will mar its smoothness when unmolded. Cover with plastic wrap or foil and refrigerate until firm. Unmold on salad greens. Needs no dressing. 6 servings.

FISH CREOLE

1 small onion, minced
1 rib celery, chopped
1 tablespoon minced parsley
1 clove garlic, minced
¼ cup margarine, melted
2½ cups canned tomatoes
1½ cups mushrooms, sliced
1 bay leaf
1 tablespoon sugar

pepper to taste
2 dashes Tabasco
½ cup tomato paste
1½ pounds haddock or cod
  fillets
1 tablespoon lemon juice
salt to taste
1 teaspoon Worcestershire sauce
1 cup rice, cooked

In a large skillet, sauté onion, celery, parsley and garlic in half the margarine until soft. Stir in tomatoes, mushrooms, bay leaf, sugar, pepper, Tabasco and tomato paste. Bring to boil, then simmer, stirring occasionally, 15 to 20 minutes until slightly thickened. Cut fish into six servings. Combine lemon juice and remaining margarine, pour over fish; sprinkle with salt. Add fish and Worcestershire. Cook over low heat 10 minutes or until fish flakes. Serve with hot boiled rice. Recipe may be doubled. 6 servings.

HOW TO BONE A TROUT

To bone dressed, uncooked trout and keep the head and tail in place, open body cavity; insert a sharp knife at the head end under the backbone and cut between the ribs and flesh, releasing the bones from the fish back. Take care not to cut through the back of the fish. Repeat to free the other side of the backbone and rib cage. Ease backbone free, leaving back flesh on trout intact. Using kitchen shears, snip backbone at head and tail. Lift out the bony skeleton and discard. Cut off and discard fins. Fish is now ready for stuffing, or can be spread open, butterflied.

BAKED TROUT PROVENCAL

4 to 6 medium trout
(about ½ lb each)
¼ cup lemon juice
1 teaspoon salt
1 clove garlic

1 cup white wine
2 tablespoons chopped parsley
2 tablespoons chopped green onion
2 tablespoons dry bread crumbs
¼ cup (½ stick) melted margarine

Preheat oven to 400°F. Wipe pan-dressed trout dry. Rub with lemon juice, sprinkle with salt. Grease a shallow baking dish and sprinkle bottom with minced garlic. Place trout in dish in single layer. Pour wine over all. Sprinkle with parsley, green onion and crumbs. Drizzle with melted margarine. Bake in hot oven for 20 minutes. 4 to 6 servings.

OVEN CRISP TROUT

6 medium trout
salt and pepper
¼ cup soft margarine
½ cup chopped parsley
¾ cup dry fine toasted
bread crumbs

½ cup shredded Swiss cheese
1 egg
¼ cup milk
1 teaspoon salt
2 tablespoons margarine

Preheat oven to 500°F. Wash and dry pan-dressed trout, season with salt and pepper. Brush fish cavity with melted margarine and sprinkle with parsley. Blend cheese and bread crumbs; set aside. Beat eggs, milk and salt lightly. Dip each trout into milk mixture, then crumbs, coating outside well. Arrange fish on generously greased shallow baking pan. Leftover crumbs may be sprinkled over top. Dot with margarine. Bake in very hot oven 15 to 20 minutes, or until fish is browned and flakes when pierced with fork. 6 servings.

GRILLED TROUT WITH WALNUTS

4 frozen brook trout, about
   10 ounces each, thawed
1 cup walnuts, finely chopped
1 egg
½ teaspoon grated lemon rind
2 tablespoons lemon juice

2 tablespoons parsley,
   finely chopped
½ teaspoon salt
margarine
1 lemon, quartered lengthwise

Trout should be opened and cleaned but with heads left on. Mix walnuts with egg, grated lemon rind, lemon juice, parsley and salt. Stuff each fish with 3 tablespoons of nut mixture. Close opening with metal skewers. Brush fish on both sides with margarine. Grill, 6 inches above white-hot charcoal, allowing about 6 minutes for each side, or until fish flakes when tested with a fork. Serve with lemon wedges. May also be broiled in your oven. You may want to baste once with melted margarine, each side. Makes 4 servings.

This is a famous dish served often in restaurants surrounding Lake Como, Italy.

RAINBOW TROUT LAKE COMO

4 medium rainbow trout
1½ cups Italian style oil
   and vinegar salad dressing

½ cup pine nuts
½ cup (1 stick) melted margarine

Bone and butterfly four medium rainbow trout. Place in a shallow baking dish skin down. Pour over the fish the 1½ cups Italian salad dressing. Cover and marinate in refrigerator 30 minutes. Place skin down on heated grill or lightly oiled broiler pan. Broil about 10 minutes, basting occasionally with marinade until fish is moist but flakes easily. Remove to heated platter. Pour over all ½ cup melted margarine to which you have added ½ cup pine nuts. 4 servings.

ELEGANT CHILLED TROUT WITH DILL SAUCE

2 medium or 4 small rainbow trout,
  heads on but cleaned
Water to cover fish in skillet
1 medium sliced onion
6 whole black peppercorns
2 whole allspice
1 bay leaf
1 teaspoon salt
¼ cup lemon juice or white vinegar
½ cup dry white wine

½ cup sour cream
1 tablespoon lemon juice
½ teaspoon salt
¼ teaspoon dill weed
12 small pickled onions
Watercress or parsley
1 lemon cut in wedges
1 tablespoon margarine
*One 12 inch skillet with cover
  and rack or trivet to fit inside.

Bring one quart water to boil in skillet without rack or trivet in it. Into water place onion, peppercorns, allspice, bay leaf, salt, lemon juice or white vinegar. Simmer 15 minutes to develop flavor. Grease top of rack with margarine and place in skillet. Arrange trout on rack. Add white wine. Water should *almost* cover trout. If not, add more boiling water. Cover and simmer gently for 10 minutes. Using a tongs, lift out rack with trout on it. Gently remove skin, leaving on head and tail fins. Lift fish into oblong baking pan to fit. Pour poaching liquid over fish through a strainer to hold back seasoning vegetables. Refrigerate fish. To serve, arrange chilled fish on platter; decorate with watercress or parsley, lemon wedges and small pickled onions. Serve with sauce made from sour cream, lemon juice, salt and dill weed. Makes 4 servings.

Note: Any remaining poaching liquid can be strained and refrigerated for other use.

*Replaces fish kettle.

SHRIMP JAMBALAYA

1 pound cooked, shelled shrimp
1 cup chopped green pepper
½ cup chopped onion
2 cloves garlic, finely chopped
¼ cup (½ stick) melted margarine
1 (16 ounce) can tomatoes
1½ cups water

1 cup uncooked rice
½ teaspoons crushed whole
  thyme
¼ teaspoon salt
1 bay leaf
Dash pepper
¼ cup chopped parsley

Cook green pepper, onion and garlic in margarine until tender. Add remaining ingredients except shrimp and parsley. Cover and cook for 25–30 minutes or until rice is tender; stir occasionally. Add parsley and shrimp; heat. Remove bay leaf. 6 servings.

This is a pretty dish to serve from a chafing dish on the buffet. Patty shells or toast cups or toast should be on a heating tray close by. Good for after theatre entertaining.

SHRIMP CURRY

¾ pound shrimp
½ cup chopped onion
¼ cup (½ stick) margarine, melted
¼ cup flour
1 teaspoon salt
Dash pepper

1¾ cups chicken broth
  or bouillon
1½ teaspoons curry powder
½ cup apple sauce
3 cups cooked rice
Curry accompaniments

Cook onion in margarine until tender. Blend in flour, salt, and pepper. Add broth gradually and cook until thick, stirring constantly. Add curry powder, applesauce and shrimp; heat. Serve on rice with any of the following curry accompaniments. 6 servings.

Curry Accompaniments:

chopped hard cooked egg whites, sieved hard cooked egg yolks, chopped salted peanuts, chopped green onion tops, chopped tomatoes, chutney, freshly grated coconut.

Over-cooking is the danger here — scallops may be fully cooked in 15 minutes. Taste one; serve the second they're hot-through. Saves time to cook lots of rice; some to refrigerate, more to freeze. Rice reheats to perfection.

HERB-BAKED SCALLOPS

2 pounds scallops, fresh
  or frozen (thawed)
½ cup (1 stick) margarine
¼ cup chopped parsley

1 teaspoon dried thyme
1 teaspoon salt
¼ teaspoon pepper
2 cups rice, cooked

Preheat oven to 350°F. Quickly rinse scallops with cold water; drain on paper towels. Melt margarine, add parsley, thyme, salt, pepper. In shallow baking dish arrange single layer of scallops; spoon margarine mixture over scallops. Bake 5 minutes; shake pan to coat scallops on all sides with margarine. Bake 10 to 20 minutes longer — testing for doneness. Serve on heated plates with hot rice and pan sauce spooned over scallops. 6 servings.

No last minute rush — you can make up seasoned fish packets in advance and keep them refrigerated. Wonderful choice for beach or park cook-outs.

FOIL-BAKED FISH

3 pounds fresh or frozen
  halibut steak, 1 to 1½
  inches thick, or any
  comparable white, firm-
  fleshed fish or filets
5 slices of bacon, minced
1 large green pepper, minced

1 cup chopped onions
1 large red pepper, minced
1 cup sour cream
1 teaspoon salt
¼ teaspoon pepper
¼ teaspoon paprika
¼ cup (½ stick) margarine, melted

Cut fish in 4 portions. Cook bacon; Sauté pepper and onion in bacon fat until soft but not brown. Stir in sour cream and spoon over fish that has been sprinkled with salt, pepper and paprika. Tear off 4 sheets of 18-inch heavy-duty aluminum foil, each about 24 inches long. Fold each sheet in half crosswise. Brush one side with the melted margarine. Place portion of fish on the greased side of each piece of foil. Top each fish portion with a quarter of the sour cream mixture. Fold foil closed, fastening tightly. Place on grill, almost directly on top of white-hot charcoal. Grill 20 to 25 minutes. Open one packet to test fish by flaking with fork. Fillets will take less time than fish steaks. 6 to 8 servings.

SCALLOPED OYSTERS

2 cups oysters, shucked, in
  liquid
½ cup fine bread crumbs
½ cup fine cracker crumbs
½ cup (1 stick) margarine,
  melted

2 tablespoons oyster liquid
1 tablespoon milk
salt and pepper to taste

Preheat oven to 450°F. Clean the oysters for bits of shell and reserve the liquid. Mix the bread and cracker crumbs with the melted margarine. Place a thin layer of the crumb mixture in a shallow greased baking dish. Cover this layer with half the oysters. Sprinkle with salt and pepper. Top with the oyster liquid and milk. Repeat. Cover the top with the remaining crumbs. Bake for 20 minutes. 4 servings.

A good choice for days when you know you'll be late getting home for dinner. This fishbake can be prepared in advance and refrigerated. Even faster if you prepare it in a dish that can go from refrigerator to oven safely. Cover with plastic wrap or aluminum foil when refrigerated. Goes well with Swedish Beet Apple Salad.

SCANDINAVIAN FISHBAKE

1 pound perch fillets
2 tablespoons lemon juice
2 tablespoons margarine
¾ cup flavored breadcrumbs
¾ cup evaporated milk
1 (10 ounce) package frozen
   cauliflower

1 pound jar boiled onions
⅔ cup shredded cheddar cheese
lemon, parsley or fresh dill
   for garnish

Preheat oven to 350°F. Sprinkle fish with lemon juice. Grease baking pan with margarine. Sprinkle bottom with dusting of dry crumbs. Blend remaining crumbs with evaporated milk; set aside. Arrange perch cut in serving portions, cauliflower buds and drained onions in baking pan. Pour crumb-milk mixture over fish and vegetables. Cover with shredded cheese. Bake 30 to 40 minutes. Garnish with lemon, parsley or fresh dill. 4 servings.

Good organizers keep an emergency shelf or cupboard filled at all times. Contents that include sardines will save many problems . . . and get you compliments, too.

SARDINE STUFFED PEPPERS

2 (4 ounce) cans sardines in oil
4 to 6 green peppers
1 (9 ounce) package rice pilaf

½ teaspoon tumeric (optional)
2 (8 ounce) cans tomato sauce

Preheat oven to 375°F. Drain oil from sardines. Prepare peppers, boil 5 minutes and drain. Make rice pilaf according to package directions. Reserve 1 whole sardine to use later to garnish each pepper shell. Break up remaining sardines and fold into cooked rice. Fill pepper shells and top with reserved sardine. Place in greased baking dish. Pour tomato sauce over and around peppers. Bake in over for 30 minutes. 4 to 6 servings.

Great for a quick lunch on a project filled day. Good for picnics, too.

SARDINE SANDWICHES

2 (4½ ounce) can skinless, boneless
   sardines in oil
1 large red onion
8 slices thin-sliced
   pumpernickel bread

1 tablespoon margarine
Dijon style mustard
juice of ½ lemon
2 raw carrots cut in sticks
4 ribs celery cut in sticks

Remove sardines from can to plate. With fork mash well, incorporating fish oil. Peel onion, slice very thin crosswise. Spread four slices of bread with margarine. Top margarine with mustard. On remaining four slices spread sardines. Top sardines with thin onion rings, sprinkle with squeezed lemon juice. Top each with margarine-mustard spread slice. Serve with carrot and celery sticks. 2 servings.

CRUSTY BROILED HALIBUT

4 halibut steaks, 1 inch thick
   (1½ to 2 pounds)
½ cup (1 stick) margarine
   melted

1 lemon, sliced
parsley for garnish

Seasoned breadcrumbs:

1 cup fine, dry white bread crumbs rolled smooth. Mix with crumbs — dash of salt, pepper, onion salt, garlic salt, paprika, dill weed, plus 1 teaspoon grated lemon peel. Shake well before serving.

Preheat oven to 475°F. Brush shallow baking dish with some melted margarine. Arrange fish steaks in dish. Brush steaks liberally with remaining margarine. Sprinkle breadcrumbs liberally over steaks. Pat gently with fingertips or spatula so crumbs will adhere to top of steaks. Place steaks 3 inches from heat. Fish is done when it flakes easily when tested with fork. Serve additional melted margarine flavored with lemon juice and chopped parsley. 4 servings.

Note: Steaks should be 1 inch thick.

This delicious and colorful salad is an ideal dish to serve on hot days. Not only beautiful to see, but just the right amount of nourishment. Add a cold glass of iced tea and you have perfection.

SUMMERTIME SHRIMP AVOCADO SALAD

10 ounces cooked, shelled shrimp
2 tablespoons lemon juice
2 avocados, peeled and cubed

Lettuce
Lemon Cream Dressing

Sprinkle lemon juice over avocado. Chill. Line platter with lettuce. Portion avocado and shrimp on the lettuce. Top with Lemon Cream Dressing. 6 servings.

Lemon Cream Dressing

½ cup sour cream
1 tablespoon lemon juice
1 tablespoon chopped parsley

1 teaspoon horseradish
¼ teaspoon salt

Combine all ingredients and chill.

Chesapeake Bay is noted for its delicious crabs and crab cakes are a favorite along the Eastern Shore. This is an easy recipe to follow and canned crabmeat is available year round. Use fresh crab if available.

MARYLAND CRAB CAKES

1 pound crabmeat
1 cup seasoned breadcrumbs
1 large egg
About ¼ cup mayonnaise
1 teaspoon Worcestershire sauce

1 teaspoon dry mustard
½ teaspoon salt
¼ teaspoon pepper
Margarine for frying

Remove all cartilage from crabmeat. In a bowl, mix breadcrumbs, egg, mayonnaise and seasonings. Add crabmeat and mix gently but thoroughly. If mixture is too dry, add a little more mayonnaise. Shape into 6 cakes. Cook cakes in fry pan, in just enough margarine to prevent sticking, until browned; about 5 minutes on each side.

Note: If desired, crab cakes can be deep fried at 350°F for 2 to 3 minutes, or until browned.

Poultry

Without question, America's good gift to today's world is the three pound, broiler-fryer chicken that was bred in Chesapeake country in the 50's, and now is produced round the globe.

One bonus for sharing these lean, meaty birds with a protein-hungry world is the practically endless exchange of recipes for the international classics.

In France, Italy, Germany, Scandinavia, the Orient — everywhere these chickens now grow and are marketed, skilled cooks praise their versatility. And they share one major discovery: Boned breastmeat of these American chickens makes a superb stand-in for European veal.

The most economical buy is the whole chicken that you carry home and bone in minutes. Or roast the whole chicken — or two of them — with stuffing and serve with giblet gravy at dinner. Goes well with a glass of your favorite white or rosé wine!

1 whole chicken, about 3 pounds	¼ cup (½ stick) margarine
½ lemon	

Rinse chicken inside and out, carefully removing bag of giblets and neck in cavity of bird. (Set aside giblet bag to use contents later for making homemade chicken broth.) Rub chicken inside and out with lemon. Set bird aside. Keep margarine at room temperature.

Make stuffing. Very, very loosely fill body cavity and neck with stuffing (or bake stuffing in separate foil package alongside chicken during last 30 minutes of roasting). Unstuffed bird may have slices of onion, celery tops and ½ teaspoon dried tarragon, thyme or sage placed in cavity before roasting. No need to close cavity or bird with skewers, open cavity permits better heat penetration into the very center. Fold wings underneath bird — wings akimbo — and over neck skin. Loosely tie legs to keep them straight — for appearance only. Rub bird with soft margarine for a crisp, golden and flavorful skin. Place uncovered bird in roasting pan on middle rack of 375°F oven.

Roast about 90 minutes, until leg will move up and down readily. Or press fleshy part of drumstick with fingers protected with a paper towel. 6 servings.

Bird carves more easily if allowed to stand 15 to 30 minutes. Lift chicken onto serving platter; keep warm in oven. Use roasting pan to make gravy of drippings, brown particles in pan and homemade chicken broth. Add finely chopped (cooked) giblets if you like.

Stuffing

½ cup (1 stick) margarine	1 teaspoon thyme, tarragon
1 onion, thinly sliced	or sage
½ cup water	3 cups dry breadcrumbs
2 ribs celery, thinly sliced	½ teaspoon salt
¼ cup chopped parsley	freshly ground pepper

Melt margarine over moderate heat, add onion slices, water and celery. Cook until vegetables are limp but not brown. Add parsley, thyme, bread crumbs, salt, pepper and toss all together. Taste for salt. Stuffing will be moist, not soggy. Place very, very loosely in chicken. Extra stuffing may be foil-wrapped and baked during last 30 minutes of roasting.

Giblet Gravy

Rinse neck and giblets (found inside bag in chicken cavity) and add to saucepan with 1½ cups water or half water and half dry white wine. Add 1 teaspoon salt, 4 peppercorns, 2 cloves, slices of onion, carrots, celery tops. Bring to boil, cover, reduce heat and simmer 1 hour. Remove neck and giblets to cutting board. Finely cut meat to add later to gravy. When chicken has been removed from roasting pan, place pan over moderate heat, estimate — or measure fat in pan and reserve 2 tablespoons fat. Stir in 2 tablespoons flour then very gradually stir in chicken broth from saucepan. Boil, stirring until gravy is smooth and the thickness you desire, adding water if necessary. Taste for salt. Stir in giblets and heat. Serve in preheated gravy boat or bowl. 2 cups gravy.

Homemade Chicken Broth

Inside that bag in the cavity of a whole chicken are the neck and giblets: the liver, heart and gizzard — nutritious flavorful meat to simmer with a teaspoon of salt, some celery leaves, sprigs of parsley, 2 small onions stuck with 2 cloves, 6 peppercorns. Cover with 1 cup water, or half water and half white wine if you like, and bring to boil. Cover pan, reduce heat to low and simmer one hour or longer. This is broth to use in cooking rice, broth to make superb gravy. Chop giblets and meat (removed from neck) and add to rice or gravy, best made in roasting pan using pan drippings.

This is more delicious reheated so make it ahead if you like. Serve with rice or noodles and a big green salad — Chianti wine.

CHICKEN CACCIATORE

2 tablespoons margarine
3-pound broiler-fryer chicken, cut up
1 each onion and green pepper, sliced
1 garlic clove, minced
1 (16-ounce) can tomatoes

1 teaspoon each salt, sugar
¼ teaspoon each pepper, ground allspice
1 bay leaf
dash hot pepper sauce

Preheat oven to 375°F. Melt margarine in 10-inch skillet over moderate heat; add chicken pieces and brown well on all sides; remove to 2-quart casserole. To skillet drippings add the sliced onion, green pepper and garlic; cook until onion is soft. Drain tomatoes (save juice for another use) then chop tomatoes and add to skillet. Stir in salt, sugar, pepper, ground allspice, bay leaf and hot pepper sauce. Heat to boiling then pour over chicken in casserole and bake in oven about 45 minutes, until chicken is tender. 4 servings.

CHICKEN A LA KING

2 tablespoons margarine
½ green pepper, shredded
1 cup thinly sliced mushrooms
2 tablespoons flour
salt and pepper
2 cups light cream
3 cups cut-up chicken, cooked
¼ cup (½ stick) margarine,
    creamed

3 egg yolks
1 teaspoon onion juice
1 tablespoon lemon juice
½ teaspoon paprika
sherry
1 pimiento, shredded

Simmer margarine, green pepper and mushrooms 5 minutes. Add flour and seasonings. Cook, stirring gently until frothy. Add cream and stir until sauce is thickened. Pour into top of double boiler. Add chicken; heat thoroughly over hot water. Beat the creamed margarine into the egg yolks. Add onion juice, lemon juice and paprika. Add slowly to hot chicken mixture, stirring until thickened. Add pimiento. Serve immediately in croustades — little bread cases — or on hot buttered toast. 8 servings.

Croustades

24 slices very fresh white
    bread, thinly sliced

¼ cup (½ stick) margarine
    at room temperature

Preheat oven to 375°F. Cut each slice of bread in 3-inch rounds, using cookie cutter. Spread each completely with the margarine, then fit the rounds, margarine side down, into tiny, 2-inch muffin cups. Gently press bread to fit neatly and form little cups. Place in oven and bake 3 to 5 minutes, until bread is crisp but not browned. Watch. Remove immediately from tins and cool. Pack or freeze. Yield: 24 croustades.

EASY FOIL-WRAPPED CHICKEN

Cut-up chicken for 2 to 8 people
Margarine

Salt and pepper
Plenty of foil

Preheat oven to 350°F. Rinse and dry chicken; rub generously with margarine, salt and pepper. And if you like add Italian seasoning, crushed tarragon or thyme, parsley flakes, onion or garlic powder, some hickory smoke salt. Place on foil and wrap with tight seal. Arrange on baking sheet and bake in oven about 45 minutes; test by cutting to the bone of one piece. Juice will run clear, not pink. Serve hot or cold.

BACHELOR'S CHICKEN

2 broiler-fryer chickens in
   quarters, about 6 pounds in all
salt and pepper

½ cup (1 stick) margarine
1½ cups sour cream

Rinse and dry chicken then sprinkle generously with salt, pepper. Let rest while preheating oven to slow — 250°F. Place casserole containing margarine in oven to melt it. Roll chicken in soft margarine. Bake 1½ hours, basting a couple of times. Test for doneness. Shortly before serving, pour off some of the gravy and mix with sour cream and return to casserole just to heat through. 8 servings.

ROAST TURKEY BREAST WITH CURRIED FRUIT

1 frozen (4 pound) turkey breast
   salt, pepper
¼ cup (½ stick) margarine
½ teaspoon each ground ginger,
   coriander

2 (29-ounce) cans peach or
   pear halves
2 cups uncooked long grain rice

Sauce

½ cup (1 stick) margarine
1 cup chopped fresh apple
½ cup chopped onion
2 cloves garlic, minced

½ cup flour
2 teaspoons curry powder
2 cups chicken consommé or bouillon
1 cup milk

Preheat oven to 350°F. Thaw turkey breast, rinse, dry and sprinkle meat with salt, pepper. Place in foil-lined roasting pan. Melt margarine in saucepan with ginger and coriander then use to brush both sides of turkey breast. Roast in oven 1½ hours, basting once with margarine. Drain canned fruit and place fruit in pan drippings around turkey.

Roast 20 minutes longer. Cook rice according to package directions while turkey roasts.

Make sauce by melting margarine in skillet, add chopped apple, onion and garlic and cook until soft but not brown. Add sprinkling of flour and curry; mix well. Slowly stir in chicken bouillon and milk; cook, stirring, until sauce boils and thickens. Taste sauce to adjust seasoning.

To serve, use one large platter (or two small ones). At one end of platter place turkey breast with curry sauce spooned over, then make mound of rice surrounded with the hot fruit. 8 servings.

Do these outdoors on the grill while guests watch and sip a cool, cool Kir: tablespoon of creme de cassis (black currant liqueur) in stemmed glass then partially filled with dry white wine. A twist of lemon peel on each glass, if you like.

CRUSTY BROILED DRUMSTICKS

1 cup (2 sticks) margarine
1 teaspoon dried tarragon or
  chopped parsley
1 tablespoon chopped chives or
  scallions

salt and freshly ground black
  pepper
12 chicken drumsticks

Melt margarine then stir in tarragon and chives, salt and pepper. Dip each drumstick into margarine and then arrange on foil-lined shallow baking pan; or place on charcoal grill over hot coals. Brush drumsticks with more of the margarine while they broil, turning them to brown evenly. Takes about 45 minutes. 6 servings.

Italian for "jump into the mouth" for saltimbocca is so delicious you can barely resist taking a bite of meat — right from the skillet

SALTIMBOCCA

3 whole chicken breasts
6 thin slices country ham
¼ cup freshly grated
  Parmesan cheese
¼ cup flour
1 teaspoon salt

½ teaspoon powdered sage
¼ teaspoon pepper
½ cup (1 stick) margarine
1½ cups chicken consommé
½ cup dry white wine

Chicken breasts first are skinned, boned and cut in half to make 6 cutlets. Carefully slice again to make 12 thin cutlets. Sandwich a slice of ham between 2 cutlets and fasten with toothpicks. Repeat. Mix cheese, flour, salt, sage and pepper and dip cutlets, pressing firmly to coat both sides. Shake off excess. Refrigerate. Reserve ¼ cup of the coating mixture.

In 10-inch skillet heat margarine over moderate heat, sauté cutlets — 3 or 4 at a time — about 5 minutes per side. Drain cutlets on paper towels and keep warm.

Pour off all but about ¼ cup pan drippings, add ¼ cup coating mixture, consommé and wine. Stir and cook until sauce boils and thickens. Serve saltimbocca on heated platter and pour sauce over top. More grated Parmesan if you like. 6 servings.

Italian dish cooked "mezza cottura" — over relatively high heat to brown the chicken quickly and seal in juices. Serve with broccoli, crusty hot garlic bread and glasses of Italy's chilled white soave wine. Zabaglione dessert with sliced peaches, fresh or frozen.

SCALLOPINE CON LIMONE

3 whole chicken breasts
½ cup flour
1½ teaspoons salt
½ teaspoon pepper

½ cup (1 stick) margarine
⅓ cup lemon juice
1 teaspoon grated lemon rind
¼ cup chopped parsley

Chicken breasts first are skinned, boned and cut in half to make 6 cutlets. Mix flour, salt and pepper; dip cutlets in mixture and press firmly to coat. Shake off excess. Refrigerate. In 12-inch skillet heat margarine until it bubbles; sauté cutlets 3 or 4 at a time, about 3 minutes per side. Drain on paper towels and keep warm. When all cutlets are cooked, stir lemon juice into drippings and scrape bottom to loosen brown particles. When hot, not yet boiling, pour sauce over heated platter of cutlets and top with lemon rind-parsley mixture. 6 servings.

It takes under an hour to prepare and cook this chicken with sauce. Serve over boiled rice and pass the condiments: chopped peanuts, raisins, chutney, sliced bananas.

CHICKEN CURRY WITH APPLES

3 pound broiler-fryer chicken, cut up
salt, pepper
¼ cup (½ stick) margarine
3 apples, peeled and diced
½ cup finely chopped onion

2 tablespoons each curry powder
   and flour
1½ cups chicken bouillon
   or consommé

Rinse chicken, dry, rub lightly with salt, pepper. In 10-inch skillet melt margarine then add chicken and brown well on all sides, using moderate heat. Remove chicken pieces as they brown. When finished, add apples and onion to skillet. Brown and stir in curry powder and flour; cook 2 minutes. Slowly stir in chicken bouillon, stirring until it boils and thickens. Return chicken to skillet, cover and simmer 20 to 30 minutes; until chicken is tender. Serve with rice and pass bowls of condiments. 4 servings.

Do these outdoors on the grill or in the kitchen oven. Takes 2 hours, start to finish, to present this elegant fare for four.

BARBECUED CORNISH HENS — WILD RICE STUFFING

1 (6 ounce) package long-grain and
   wild rice mix
¼ cup raisins
2 tablespoons margarine
2 tablespoons slivered almonds

½ teaspoon poultry seasoning or sage
4 Rock Cornish Game hens, thawed
   in refrigerator
¼ cup (½ stick) margarine

Make stuffing by cooking rice according to package directions; stir in raisins, margarine, almonds and poultry seasoning. Rinse game hens, dry, rub inside and out with salt. Skewer neck skins to back. Fill each bird with ¼ of the stuffing; cover opening with a piece of foil. Tie or skewer wings to body (to prevent burning); tie legs to tail. Brush birds with soft margarine; place on foil in center of grill over hot coals (or in shallow roasting pan in 375°F oven). Allow space between birds for heat to circulate. Grill or roast 1 hour and 15 to 30 minutes; brushing with drippings occasionally. 4 servings.

SAVORY LEMON PATS

Prepare, refrigerate, then serve atop a bowl of ice at the barbecue. Each pat is a cube of margarine with lemon, parsley etc. to melt over hot-off-the-grill chicken, beef, fish.

½ cup (1 stick) margarine
2 teaspoons grated lemon rind
3 teaspoons lemon juice
1 teaspoon salt

3 tablespoons chopped parsley
⅛ teaspoon each thyme and
   tarragon

Cream margarine then gradually add the seasonings. Cream constantly to blend ingredients and flavors. Shape in a roll; wrap snugly; refrigerate. Cut in pats — and serve over hot grilled or broiled meat or fish. Makes 12 pats.

PRIZE LEMON-BROILED CHICKEN

2 broiler-fryer chickens,
  3 pounders cut in halves
1 large lemon
½ cup (1 stick) margarine, melted
2 teaspoons salt

½ teaspoon freshly ground
  black pepper
½ teaspoon paprika
2 tablespoons sugar

Rinse chicken, then rub dry. Carefully rub chicken inside and out with lemon quarters to release all the juice; brush with melted margarine. Mix together salt, pepper, paprika and sugar; sprinkle over chickens. Place skin side down in broiler pan and place very low down in broiler. After 30 minutes turn chickens, baste with more of the sauce, and raise closer to heat. Baste and watch for even browning. Takes 20 to 30 minutes longer, until juices run clear when meat is cut to the bone. 4 large servings.

Tender cutlets are topped with eggplant slice, mozzarella, pizza sauce, grated Parmesan cheese and broiled for 5 minutes. Serve with favorite pasta, spinach salad, California Zinfandel in the carafe.

CHICKEN PARMIGIANA

3 whole chicken breasts
2 eggs (slightly beaten)
1½ teaspoons salt
½ teaspoon pepper
2 cups dry breadcrumbs

1 cup (2 sticks) margarine
6 slices eggplant, ½-inch thick
1½ cups pizza sauce
6 slices Mozzarella cheese
¼ cup grated Parmesan cheese

Chicken breasts first are skinned, boned and cut in half to make 6 cutlets. Combine eggs, salt and pepper; coat meat, then dip into crumbs and press to coat evenly. Arrange in single layer and refrigerate 10 minutes. In 10-inch skillet heat 1 stick margarine to bubbling. Sauté cutlets — 3 or 4 at a time — about 3 minutes per side. Drain on paper towels and keep warm. Melt second stick of margarine in pan and sauté eggplant slices until golden. Sprinkle with salt, pepper. Arrange cutlets on heat-proof serving platter; top each with slice of eggplant, ribbon of pizza sauce and slice of Mozzarella. Sprinkle with grated Parmesan. Broil 6 inches from heat about 5 minutes — to melt cheese. 6 servings.

STUFFED TURKEY DRUMSTICKS AND ARTICHOKES

8 turkey drumsticks (about
   8 pounds)
salt, pepper
2 pounds Italian sausage, sweet
   or hot
½ cup (1 stick) margarine
1 bunch scallions, chopped to make
   1½ cups

⅓ cup flour
1 (32-ounce) can tomatoes
½ cup sliced stuffed or black olives
½ cup dry wine, red or white
8 small artichokes
2 tablespoons lemon juice

Preheat oven to 350°F. Using sharp knife with short blade, slash drumstick lengthwise, cutting meat to the bone. Open meat and spread to release bone; pull bone out. Remove tough, bone-like tendons. Place meat on table, skin-side down. Take sausage from casing and use to stuff turkey meat. Fold turkey in drumstick shape again and tie with string. Place in foil-lined roasting pan. Roast 2 hours, until drumsticks are fork-tender. Baste once with pan drippings.

In skillet melt margarine, add scallions and cook until soft. Sprinkle on flour; stir, then add juice drained from canned tomatoes and stir until sauce boils and thickens. Add chopped canned tomatoes, sliced olives and wine; stir until it boils. Taste to adjust seasoning.

To cook artichokes:

wash and trim, cutting off top-ends of leaves. Cook in 3-inches boiling water with lemon juice added. Cover and boil about 30 minutes, until fork-tender. Drain. Use spoon to scoop out thistlelike choke in center.

To serve, untie drumsticks then arrange on heated platter with a bit of the sauce spooned over. Surround with artichokes, filling centers with remaining sauce. 8 servings.

SEASONING SALT FOR CHICKEN

1 cup salt
1 tablespoon sugar
3 tablespoons paprika
2 teaspoons freshly ground
   black pepper

1 teaspoon celery salt
dash of cayenne pepper

Shake all ingredients in covered jar. Use instead of salt to flavor and color broiled or roast chicken.

Meats

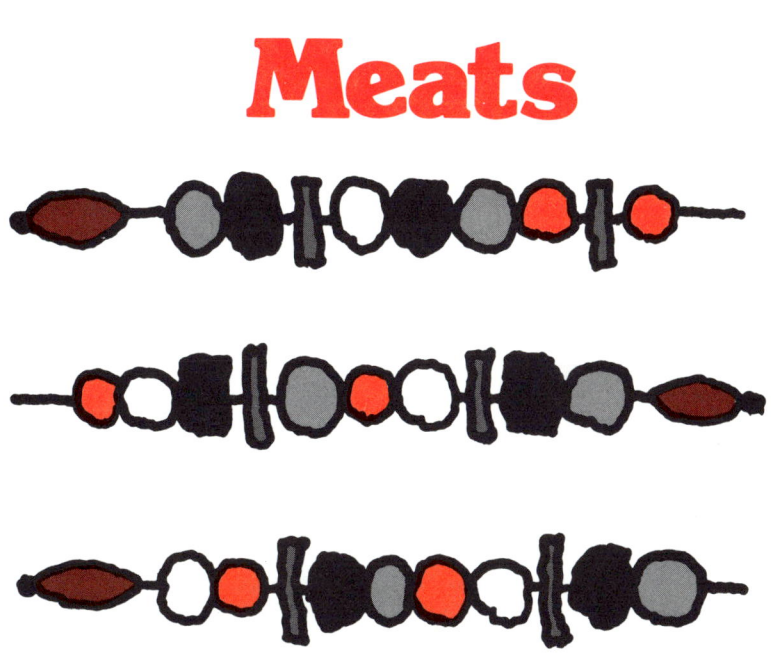

Meat is so basic that, in our language, we use "meat" to mean the central point — "the meat of the matter." It appears on our dining tables at breakfast, lunch and dinner, and comes on very plain or very elegant — very expensive or very economical — as the occasion demands.

It can be served in almost every imaginable way, and is compatible with almost every other kind of food and drink. In some parts of the world, the Mideast, for example, the most available meat dominates the menus (in that case, lamb). But, in the United States there is no limit to the variety of meats offered, and we are encouraged to try new tastes and textures.

To get to the meat of the matter, meat is one of our most important sources of protein — essential for body building and repair, whether it comes from Daube Glacé or Red Flannel Hash.

This elegant French Pot Roast of Beef is the perfect spotlight for your party table. Spectacular to see and delicious to taste. Fortunately for you busy couples it can be made ahead . . . no, *must* be made ahead. If "HE" likes to cook, this dish is for him. Not quick slap dash, but worth the effort.

DAUBE GLACÉ

3 to 4 pounds lean beef pot roast.
　(Brisket is good)
2 tablespoons margarine
2 tablespoons salad oil
Salt and black pepper
1 teaspoon coriander, ground
2 cloves garlic, sliced
1 large onion, coarsely chopped

6 whole cloves
1 bayleaf
2 cups red wine
Water
3 envelopes unflavored gelatin
3 beef bouillon cubes
parsley, mushrooms, olives etc.
　for garnish

In a heavy roasting pot with a cover, brown meat on all sides in margarine and oil. Sprinkle with salt, black pepper and coriander. Surround meat with garlic, onion, cloves, bayleaf. Pour over it 1 cup of wine and 1 cup of water. Heat liquids to boiling point then cover and reduce to simmer. Now you can set out the ingredients for the glacé, or gelatin, because the meat will have to cook slowly about 3 hours. Test occasionally with fork and add more water if needed.

When the meat is done, remove it from the pot, cool, then chill before slicing. Wet a square of double cheesecloth and wring out. Spread it over a large bowl. Pour cooking liquid from your roasting pot through the cloth to strain it. Chill bowl to harden fat. Discard solidified fat. Measure cooking liquid. To it add beef bouillon made from cubes and water to total 5 cups liquid. Pour one cup of it into medium saucepan. Set aside.

Soften 3 envelopes of plain gelatin in 1 cup red wine. Add to bouillon in saucepan. Heat and stir until dissolved. Combine with remaining gravy-bouillon mixture.

After meat is sliced, arrange on platters. Two make it easier to serve from a buffet for a large group. Platters should be deep enough to hold about one inch of gelatin. Pour the gelatin over meat to completely cover. Gently separate and lift slices a bit with small spatula so gelatin can seep between. Refrigerate. Your glacé is complete.

Before serving you can decorate the platters with mushrooms, carrot curls, olives, parsley, etc.

Put out both fork and pie server to separate and lift individual slices. Makes 10 to 12 servings.

Do your advance preparation indoors where and while it is cool. This creole sauce mixture tenderizes and flavors the lamb.

CREOLE LAMB RIBS

6 pounds breast of lamb,
  bones cracked
Boiling water
1 cup chopped onion
1 clove garlic, minced
½ cup (1 stick) margarine
1 cup water
½ cup white vinegar

1 cup chili sauce
2 tablespoons lemon juice
½ cup Worcestershire sauce
½ cup firmly packed brown sugar
1 tablespoon chili powder
1 tablespoon dry mustard
Dash liquid hot-pepper
seasoning

Preheat oven to 300°F. Ribs should be precooked by placing them on rack in roasting pan. Add boiling water to depth of 1 inch. Cover pan with heavy aluminum foil. Bake for 1½ hours. Sauté onion and garlic in margarine until soft. Add the remaining ingredients. Bring to boiling; lower heat; simmer 1 hour. (This sauce may be made in advance and kept for several days in the refrigerator. Heat sauce before using on ribs). Place ribs directly on grill or thread on spit. Grill, 5 inches above white-hot charcoal for 15 minutes. Baste with sauce often for the next 20 minutes, or until done and ribs are glazed. 6 to 8 servings.

Flank steak is an excellent cut of meat. The flavor is delicious and it can be cooked many different ways.

TERIYAKI STEAK

1 flank steak 2–2½ pounds
1 cup soy sauce
1 cup dry sherry
¼ cup canned beef broth
1 teaspoon sugar

1 clove garlic, crushed
1 tablespoon preserved ginger,
  finely chopped
soy sauce

Put steak in a shallow glass or non-metal dish. Combine soy sauce, sherry, beef broth, sugar, garlic and ginger in a bowl. Pour over steak. Marinate meat in mixture for 4 hours, turning occasionally. Grill 4 inches above white-hot charcoal, allowing 5 minutes on each side for rare. Brush with the sauce several times. Cut diagonally across grain into thin slices and serve with additional soy sauce. 6–8 servings.

Lamb need not be too costly for regular family meals. This is an easy to make and tasty economical dish. The zesty seasonings enhance its taste. Patties and vegetables can be prepared ahead to speed up cooking time.

LAMB PATTIES WITH CARIBBEAN BARBECUE SAUCE

1 pound ground lamb
1 cup grated raw carrot
2 tablespoons minced onion
1 egg, slightly beaten
1 teaspoon salt

¼ teaspoon pepper
¼ teaspoon curry powder
2 tablespoons margarine
1 teaspoon Kitchen Bouquet
　or Gravy Master

Barbecue Sauce

2 tablespoons molasses
2 tablespoons prepared mustard
½ teaspoon Tabasco

2 tablespoons vinegar
1 tablespoon Worcestershire Sauce

Thoroughly blend lamb, carrot, onion, egg, salt, pepper, and curry powder. Shape into 4–6 patties. Place on broiler pan. Blend margarine and Kitchen Bouquet together. Brush patties with half this mixture. Place about 5 inches from broiler. Broil about 5 minutes. Mix sauce ingredients together. Baste patties and broil 2 more minutes. Turn patties and brush with margarine mixture and broil about 5 minutes. Then baste with sauce and broil 2 minutes. Serve with remaining sauce. 4 servings.

"Grillades" are featured in a fabulous and famous New Orleans restaurant. Use a light hand with heat and it will always turn out successfully.

"GRILLADES" . . . FROM NEW ORLEANS

2 pounds round steak cut
  ¾ inch thick
¼ cup (½ stick) margarine
1 tablespoon cooking oil
1 tablespoon flour

1 medium onion, finely chopped
1½ cups tomato juice
1 teaspoon each salt and pepper
1 clove garlic, crushed
2 cups rice, cooked

Heat margarine and oil in heavy skillet. Cut steak into individual servings; brown in skillet; remove to platter. Blend flour into oil and margarine in skillet; add onion and brown slightly over low heat. Add tomato juice slowly, stir until smooth. Replace steak, season with salt, pepper and garlic. Cover and cook slowly over low heat 60 minutes or longer, until tender. Add more liquid if necessary. Serve over fluffy white rice. 6 servings.

If you have a special liking for herbs, try adding a pinch of thyme, 2 bay leaves, or coriander. For garnish, fresh green chopped parsley adds an appetizing touch.

For the busy cook who likes good food but can't spend too much money or time cooking it, this is the perfect choice.

THRIFTY SKILLET DINNER

1 pound ground beef
¼ cup (½ stick) margarine
2 tablespoons chopped onion
¼ cup chopped green pepper

1 pound can tomatoes
salt and pepper to taste
1 teaspoon sweet basil
3 medium zucchini squash

Heat margarine in large skillet. Pinch off walnut sized pieces of beef. Place into skillet and stir gently to brown slightly. Add onion and green pepper; simmer until limp. Add tomatoes, salt, pepper and basil. Cover and cook while you slice zucchini squash. Uncover and pile squash over meat and sauce. Cover and cook 10 to 15 minutes, stirring occasionally, until squash is tender. Good with rice or mashed potatoes. 6 servings.

Southern hospitality probably got its reputation from this dish.

PLANTATION HAM AND BISCUIT

6 slices fully cooked ham,
  individual servings
1 tablespoon margarine
1 cup molasses

1 cup brown sugar
1 tablespoon margarine
fresh baked biscuits
crab apples (if desired)

Brown ham slices in 1 tablespoon margarine in large skillet. Taffy sauce: Mix molasses, brown sugar and margarine in saucepan. Cook over medium heat three or four minutes, stirring constantly. Pour half the taffy sauce over ham in skillet and simmer one or two minutes. Remove to large platter and surround with fresh baked biscuits. Pass remaining sauce at table. Decorate platter with jar of spiced crab apples, if desired. 6 servings.

Here's a quick, delicious way to cook liver. Liver strips may be cooked and refrigerated in advance to speed up preparation time.

LIVER AND ONIONS

1½ pounds beef liver
1 large onion, chopped
2 tablespoons margarine

2 tablespoons wheat germ
Salt, pepper to taste
¼ cup chopped parsley

Slice liver in strips like noodles. Sauté onion in margarine over low heat. When onions are limp and transparent add liver strips. Cook about 2 minutes stirring gently until the red color has almost disappeared. Add wheat germ and seasoning. Stir again and serve. Sprinkle with parsley. 6 servings.

Moist, tender and delicious is this baked beef-orange dish. For crusty loaf, shape on shallow pan, use ring mold, or the traditional loaf pan — or bake it again, and again using all three shapes! Herbed potato bake is good companion, uses same oven heat. Try a young Beaujolais wine with this dinner-from-the-oven.

ORANGE COUNTRY MEAT LOAF

3 slices fresh bread, crusts removed
½ cup orange juice
3 pounds ground beef
3 slices bacon, cut fine
1 tablespoon grated orange rind
1½ teaspoons salt

½ teaspoon each, pepper, garlic salt
¼ teaspoon powdered basil
½ cup chopped onion
¼ cup chopped parsley
orange slices

Preheat oven to 350°F. Soak bread in orange juice 10 minutes. Combine with remaining ingredients. Shape into loaf. Place in pan. Bake 1 hour. Garnish with orange slices. 10 servings.

HERBED POTATO BAKE

½ cup (1 stick) melted margarine
2 (1⅜ ounce) envelopes onion
    soup mix

1 tablespoon dry thyme
6 unpeeled raw white potatoes

Combine margarine, soup mix and thyme. Scrub potatoes, cut in ½-inch slices. Toss potato slices in margarine mixture. Arrange in shallow baking dish with overlapping slices. Pour rest of margarine over top. Cover and bake at 350°F 1 hour. 10 servings.

Wonderfully moist with good flavor. Make this, refrigerate, then bake.

APPLE SAUCE MEAT LOAF

1½ pounds ground beef
2 eggs, beaten
2 tablespoons chopped onion
2 teaspoons salt

½ teaspoon nutmeg or allspice
¾ cup rolled oats, regular or instant
1 cup apple sauce, fresh or canned

Topping

1 pared cored apple, cut in thin rings
¼ cup brown sugar

¼ teaspoon cloves
1 tablespoon water

Preheat oven to 350°F. Combine all ingredients for meat loaf. Pack into 9 inch loaf pan. Press apple rings, cut in half, into top of meat loaf. Brush thoroughly with glaze made of brown sugar, cloves and water. Wrap and refrigerate and bake when ready for use. Bake 1 hour and 15 minutes. 8 servings.

RED FLANNEL HASH

2 cups of cooked or canned
  corned beef cut in small cubes
2 tablespoons margarine
1 (1 pound) jar or can of
  sliced beets
2 cups chopped boiled potatoes*

2 teaspoons instant minced onion
salt and pepper to taste
⅓ cup milk, evaporated milk or
  beef stock
parsley, chopped for garnish
catsup, chili sauce

*You may substitute packaged instant hashed brown potatoes, cooked.

In a heavy skillet melt 2 tablespoons margarine; add corned beef, drained and chopped beets, cooked potatoes, instant minced onion, salt, pepper, and liquid. Cover and cook over slow heat 40 minutes or until browned nicely on bottom. To serve, you may fold like an omelet and turn out onto a hot platter. Or, stir so brown bits are very visible and spoon onto hot platter. Sprinkle with parsley. Have catsup or chili sauce handy. Recipe may be doubled or tripled easily. 4 to 6 servings.

Serve piping hot for breakfast, lunch or late supper.

SAUSAGES AND APPLE BISCUITS

1½ pounds cooked sausages
¾ cup sugar
⅓ cup water
4 apples
1 package refrigerator biscuit
   dough (12 biscuits)

⅓ cup brown sugar
cinnamon
2 tablespoons margarine

Preheat oven to 425°F. Heat sausages. Boil sugar and water in covered saucepan for about 3 minutes or until sugar is dissolved. Pour into 8x8 inch baking pan. Let cool. Peel, core and chop apples. Flatten biscuit dough and spread apples over half of dough. Sprinkle with brown sugar, cinnamon and dot with margarine. Cover with other half of biscuit dough. Cut into fingers. Arrange dough, cut side down in syrup in pan. Bake for 30 minutes, or until top is golden brown. Serve topped with syrup from bottom of pan. 6 servings.

Variations:

substitute 1 cup seedless raisins, 1 cup crushed pineapple, or 4 peaches for the 4 apples.

TEENY WEENY QUICKY

2 tablespoons margarine
2 tablespoons chopped onion
¼ cup diced celery
¼ cup diced green pepper

2 tablespoons flour
1 pound can tomatoes
salt and pepper to taste
1 pound teeny weeny franks

Heat margarine in skillet. Simmer onion, celery, and green pepper until soft but not brown. Sprinkle on flour and stir until absorbed. Add tomatoes slowly, stirring constantly. Add salt and pepper to taste; simmer 10 minutes, covered. Add franks and simmer 10 minutes longer. Speed hint: Sauce may be made ahead and frozen until needed. Serve over toasted English muffins. 6 to 8 servings.

The fragrance of this hearty dinner floating through the kitchen will bring back memories of happy family days. Be prepared for compliments and requests for more. Grandma always was.

GRANDMA'S PORK CHOP BAKE

6 porkchops, about 1 inch thick
½ teaspoon salt
½ teaspoon sage
1 tablespoon margarine
5 tablespoons flour

2 cups apple juice
1 tablespoon vinegar
⅓ cup seedless raisins
3 tart apples, cored, sliced
3 tablespoons molasses

Preheat oven to 375°. Sprinkle pork chops with salt and sage. Brown in margarine. Arrange in baking dish. Add flour to skillet; cook and stir 'til browned. Add apple juice slowly, stirring constantly, and cook until mixture thickens. Add vinegar and raisins to sauce. Arrange apple slices on top of chops. Pour molasses and sauce over chops and apples. Cover and bake for 45 to 60 minutes, or until pork is done. 6 servings.

MINTED LAMB CHOPS

8 lamb chops, cut 1½ inches thick
    (about 4 pounds)
¾ cup margarine (1½ sticks); melted
2 tablespoons lemon juice

1 clove garlic, crushed
1 teaspoon salt
½ cup mint jelly, melted

Place chops in a shallow glass or other non-metal dish. Combine margarine, lemon juice, garlic and salt in a bowl; pour over chops. Marinate for 2 hours. Place chops on grill, 6 inches above white hot charcoal. Grill 8–10 minutes. Turn; grill another 8–10 minutes for medium-rare meat. Brush melted mint jelly over chops for last 2 minutes of grilling. Turn back to first side and brush jelly there too. Serve with additional mint jelly on the side, if desired. 8 servings.

This recipe once won a contest for economy, speed, flavor and general family appreciation. A perfect choice for younger members of your family to cook themselves, or a breeze for you to make for them.

EASYGOING PORK 'N' SPAGHETTI SUPPER

4 lean loin pork chops
½ teaspoon salt
1 minced clove garlic
1 minced small onion
½ chopped green pepper
1 (1 pound, 13 ounces) can tomatoes
1 (1½ ounce) package
   spaghetti sauce mix

1 tablespoon brown sugar
1 tablespoon vinegar or
   lemon juice
4 ounces thin, broken spaghetti,
   cooked

Trim fat from pork chops. Using some of this fat, brown pork chops well on both sides in a large skillet. Add garlic, onion and green pepper; cook for a few minutes. Add the tomatoes, spaghetti sauce mix, brown sugar and vinegar. Cover; simmer for 45 minutes. Add cooked spaghetti and heat to serving temperature. 4 servings.

Cranberries are a subtle flavoring and a good tenderizer. With this one hot dish add a salad and your family will be delighted.

SLICED CRANBERRY POT ROAST

1 pound top-round beef steak,
   cut ½–¾ inch thick
2 tablespoons margarine
1 tablespoon flour
1 cup jellied cranberry
   sauce, mashed

½ cup water
1 tablespoon sugar
½ teaspoon salt
3 medium potatoes, pared
   and quartered

Trim fat from beef; cut into 4 equal portions. In margarine, sauté the meat until brown over low heat. Blend the flour into margarine in pan. Add cranberry sauce, water, sugar and salt. Cover; simmer gently for 30 minutes. Then turn meat and add potatoes. Cook an hour longer or until meat and potatoes are tender. Serve with gravy from pan. 4 servings.

PORK PIE WITH SWEET POTATO BISCUITS

2½ cups diced roast lean pork
3 cooked carrots, diced
6 small cooked onions
1 tablespoon chopped parsley
6 tablespoons margarine
6 tablespoons flour

1½ cups milk
1½ cups chicken stock made
   with bouillon cube
½ teaspoon salt
dash of pepper
¼ teaspoon grated nutmeg

Preheat oven to 350°F. Place pork and vegetables in oblong baking dish. In a medium saucepan melt the margarine over low heat. Stir in the flour. Blend well. Stir in combined milk and chicken stock. Stir constantly as it cooks over low heat for about 2 minutes. A wire whisk is a helpful utensil for this. Season with salt and pepper. Add nutmeg. Pour sauce over pork and vegetables. Top with Sweet Potato Biscuit. Bake for 30 to 35 minutes. Makes 6 servings.

Sweet Potato Biscuits

1 cup flour
½ teaspoon salt
2 teaspoons baking powder

1 cup cooked mashed sweet potatoes
⅓ cup melted margarine
1 egg, beaten

Sift dry ingredients together. Combine sweet potatoes, melted margarine and beaten egg. Add dry ingredients. Mix lightly just to blend. Drop biscuits from spoon onto top of meat mixture.

Casseroles

Casserole cooking owes much to men, especially to two far-out inventors of these portable, good-to-eat dinners in a dish.

Far back in time, A Bedouin pastoral nomad took along several sheep's stomachs filled with milk for refreshment on a long trek by camel in the Arabian dessert. With all the heat and jouncing, by nightfall that milk had changed to curds and whey. The Bedouin slit open the sheep's stomach "casserole" and everyone had cheese for dinner.

More recently, a Canadian Mountie on a long drive home after a meeting on conserving energy — especially heat sources — was thoughtful. Where is heat wasted in a car? For his next long drive he triple-wrapped the meat for dinner and put it on the exhaust manifold, to ride along for the trip. Half-way there he pulled into a filling station and asked the attendant, "Will you check the oil — and please turn the roast."

(See recipe for Deviled Drumsticks To Go.)

Serve bubbling hot with marinated green bean and celery salad, crusty bread. Serve with lemon cake pudding dessert.

BARBECUE-BAKED BEANS AND BACON

2 (16 ounce) cans pork and beans
¾ cup brown sugar, packed
1 teaspoon dry mustard

8 slices bacon, cut in
  small pieces
1 cup catsup

Preheat oven to 375°F. Empty one can of beans into 1½-quart casserole. Combine brown sugar and mustard; sprinkle half this mixture over beans. Top with second can of beans; sprinkle with remaining brown sugar and mustard. Spread bacon pieces over top. Pour catsup over all. Add more bacon and ham pieces, if desired. Bake uncovered about 45 minutes, until bacon is crisp and beans bubbling hot. 8 servings.

Baked ham second-time-round is festive when baked in ring mold, the center heaped with snow-white baked grits. Serve salad of orange and onion rings, spears of romaine, oil and vinegar dressing.

PARTY HAM RING

2 eggs, lightly beaten
1 teaspoon dry mustard
few drops hot pepper sauce
3 cups soft breadcrumbs
5 cups ground cooked ham

1 (6-ounce) can frozen orange
  juice, thawed and undiluted
⅓ cup brown sugar, packed
¼ teaspoon ground cloves

Preheat oven to 350°F. Combine all ingredients; mix well. Spoon into greased 10-cup ring mold; gently pat down. Bake 1 hour. Unmold onto serving platter and heap center with baked grits, or creamed spinach, whipped potatoes or green peas and tiny onions. 8 servings.

Fresh fillets are rolled around seasoned stuffing and quickly baked. Serve with herb sauce, parslied boiled potatoes and any green vegetable in season. Pinot Chardonnay, chilled white wine is delicious with this.

NEW BEDFORD FLOUNDER CASSEROLE

2 pounds flounder fillets,
    fresh or frozen
8 slices bacon, diced
½ cup (1 stick) margarine (some set
    aside for brushing fish roll-ups)

4 cups packaged seasoned
    stuffing mix
½ teaspoon dried tarragon

Preheat oven to 375°F. Thaw frozen fillets. Cook bacon until crisp; crumble and set aside. Measure ¼ cup of the bacon fat and return to skillet with margarine and stuffing mix. Toss and add bacon, tarragon and enough hot water just to moisten — add water gradually and not too much! Place a spoonful of stuffing on each fillet; roll up firmly. Line baking pan with foil; grease foil; place roll-ups on foil in pan. Brush with melted margarine. Bake uncovered 20 minutes, until fish begins to flake when touched with a fork. Should be very moist. Serve on heated platter; pass hot Herb Sauce. 8 servings.

HERB SAUCE FOR SEAFOOD

¼ cup (½ stick) margarine
3 tablespoons lemon juice
1 tablespoon chopped parsley

½ teaspoon each basil and thyme
¼ teaspoon salt
dash of hot pepper sauce

Melt margarine. Add remaining ingredients. Keep warm 15 minutes or longer before serving. Makes ½ cup sauce.

Students from all over the world go to Harvard Business School, where this baked souffle-like cheese dish is the recipe they ask for. Rich flavor, creamy texture, it will "hold" 45 minutes on buffet hot-tray. Serve with Canadian bacon and a green salad with dressing of oil, vinegar and horseradish.

HARVARD CHEESE FONDUE

2 cups cold milk
2 cups cubed firm-type white bread,
    crusts removed
½ pound sharp Cheddar cheese,
    finely cut or grated
2 tablespoons margarine, melted

½ teaspoon dry mustard
1 teaspoon salt
few drops hot pepper sauce
6 egg yolks, lightly beaten
6 egg whites, beaten stiff
    but not dry

Preheat oven to 300°F. In cold milk soak bread cubes. Add cheese, margarine, salt, mustard and hot pepper sauce. Stir in egg yolks being careful not to crush bread cubes. Carefully fold in beaten egg whites. Pour into greased shallow 2-quart dish. Bake in slow oven until firm in the center, 45 to 60 minutes. Test for doneness: Center will feel firm to touch when pressed lightly with finger tips. Serve hot. 8 servings.

BAKED GRITS

1 cup regular or quick-cooking grits
½ cup (1 stick) margarine, cut-up
3 eggs, beaten

⅓ cup plus 2 tablespoons milk
½ pound grated sharp Cheddar
    cheese

Preheat oven to 350°F. Cook grits according to package directions. Stir margarine into grits. Combine eggs, milk, and cheese; stir into hot grits. Pour into greased shallow 2-quart baking dish. Bake 40 minutes or longer, until set. Knife blade inserted in center will come out clean. 8 servings.

All you clever men and women cooks who plan for leftovers will welcome this recipe. It's a great answer to "what will I do with this two cups of leftover beef, ham, steak, chicken, pork roast, turkey, etc., etc."

SHORTCUT SHEPHERD'S PIE

2 cups leftover meat, cut in cubes
1 (10-ounce) package mixed
  frozen vegetables
1 tablespoon instant minced onion
1 package (¾ ounces) instant cream
  gravy mix

4 servings instant mashed potato,
  prepared
2 square slices process American
  cheese, cut in half triangles

Cook frozen vegetables as package directs; when done, remove to bowl with slotted spoon and add instant onions. In vegetable water in the same saucepan make up cream gravy using package directions, adding more water if needed. Prepare four servings instant mashed potato using package directions. Set out 4 individual casseroles. In large bowl, lightly mix cooked vegetables, 2 cups cubed meat, and cream gravy. Spoon into casseroles, top each with serving of mashed potato, place ½ cheese slice on each. Broil about 4 inches from heat just to melt cheese, about 3–4 minutes. 4 servings.

SPAGHETTI, BEEF AND BEAN CASSEROLE

4 ounces spaghetti, cooked
¼ cup (½ stick) margarine
1 onion, chopped
1 green pepper, chopped
½ cup freshly grated cheese

1 (16 ounce) can red kidney beans
½ pound ground beef
1½ teaspoons salt
few drops red pepper sauce
1 (8-ounce) can tomato sauce

Preheat oven to 350°F. Cook spaghetti. Heat margarine in skillet; add onion and green pepper; cook until soft but not brown. Add all but 2 tablespoons of the cheese, the beans and liquid, ground beef, seasoning and tomato sauce (undiluted), and spaghetti. Heat to boiling; pour into 1-quart casserole and sprinkle with remaining cheese. Bake about 20 minutes 4 servings.

Cheese, kidney beans and rice provide ample protein in this very good meatless dish.

STUFFED GREEN PEPPERS

8 large green peppers
1 (16 ounce) can tomatoes
1 large onion, chopped
3 tablespoons margarine
1 cup rice, cooked
1 (20 ounce) can red kidney beans,
　drained (or use white cannellini)

12 ounce sharp Cheddar cheese,
　shredded
1 clove garlic, minced
¼ teaspoon each dried basil
　and oregano
1 teaspoon salt
dash hot pepper sauce

Preheat oven to 350°F. Cut top slice off peppers; remove seeds; parboil in boiling water 3 minutes; drain and stand upside down on paper. Drain tomatoes, reserving juice. Sauté onion in margarine until onion is soft. Add chopped tomatoes and heat through. Remove from heat. Add remaining ingredients and mix well. Stand peppers upright in deep baking dish; fill with mixture and add 1 tablespoon of tomato juice to each stuffed pepper. Cover and bake 30 minutes. If desired, uncover and brush with margarine the last 5 minutes of baking. 8 servings.

Moist and tender, with a zingy flavor — serve with plain rice and a fresh spinach salad.

PORK CHOP CACCIATORE

6 pork chops
1 large onion, sliced
2 tablespoons brown sugar

1 (1½ ounce) envelope spaghetti-
　sauce mix
2 (16-ounce) cans tomatoes

Preheat oven to 350°F. Brown chops in large skillet, then arrange in shallow 2-quart casserole. Top with onion rings and brown sugar. Using skillet and pan drippings, blend sauce mix and canned tomatoes; heat to boiling. Spoon around chops; cover. Bake 1 hour; uncover and bake 15 minutes longer. 6 servings.

Intimate dinner at home is leisurely, delightful and fragrant with aromas of pork, cornbread stuffing and good brown gravy.

STUFFED PORK CHOPS FOR TWO

4 thick pork chops, cut with pocket
1 tablespoon margarine
½ cup each chopped onion, celery
1 (7 ounce) package cornbread
   stuffing mix

1 (8 ounce) can whole kernel
   corn, drained
1 (¾ ounce) package brown
   gravy mix

Preheat oven to 350°F. Brown pork chops in margarine; turn chops and add chopped onions and celery, using moderate heat. Sauté until vegetables are soft. From stuffing package, remove vegetable seasoning packet and crumbs. Combine 2 tablespoons of the vegetable seasoning with liquid drained from canned corn and water added to make 1 cup; stir to blend. Add half of stuffing crumbs, onion, celery and corn; blend well.
(Package remaining crumbs and seasoning for future use.)
Fill pocket of each chop with stuffing; arrange in greased shallow baking dish. Spoon extra stuffing around chops. Prepare gravy mix according to package directions; pour over pork and stuffing. Cover and bake 1½ hours, until chops are fork-tender. 2 servings.

Delicious luncheon dish or first course at a barbeque, this is a bubbling beauty — with golden croutons, green chilis and cheese.

ZUCCHINI CASSEROLE

7 cups small zucchini, cut into
 ¼ inch slices
4 eggs
1 cup milk
1 teaspoon salt
2 teaspoons baking powder
¼ cup flour
¼ cup chopped parsley

1 onion, chopped
1 (4 ounce) can green chilis,
 diced
4 cups shredded Cheddar cheese
 (about ¾ pound)
1 cup soft bread cubes
¼ cup (½ stick) margarine, melted

Preheat oven to 350°F. Prepare zucchini. Beat together eggs, milk, salt, baking powder and flour until smooth. Stir in parsley, onion, green chilis, cheese and zucchini. Pour into greased 9 by 13 inch baking dish. Toss bread cubes in melted margarine then sprinkle on top. Bake uncovered 30 to 40 minutes, until center is set and zucchini is fork-tender. 10 servings.

DEVILED EGGS IN NOODLE NEST

1 (16-ounce) package medium
 noodles
½ cup (1 stick) margarine
2 cups milk
½ cup shredded Swiss cheese
6 eggs, hard-cooked

1 teaspoon spicy mustard, from jar
1 teaspoon Worcestershire Sauce
½ teaspoon salt
Dash of hot pepper sauce
2 to 3 tablespoons mayonnaise

Preheat oven to 350°F. Cook noodles according to package directions; drain; place in greased 13 by 9-inch shallow baking dish. In small saucepan melt margarine, stir in milk and shredded cheese; pour over noodles; toss to mix. Shell eggs then cut lengthwise and remove yolks. Mash yolks with seasonings, adding enough mayonnaise to make mixture creamy. Spoon into egg whites and place atop noodles in casserole. Bake 20 to 30 minutes, until golden on top. Serve hot. 6 servings.

Easy, no-watch dinner in a dish — and delicious! Serve with green salad, some red apples slices tossed in at the last minute and lemon, oil and chopped mint dressing.

HEARTY LAMB CASSEROLE

3 tablespoons margarine
8 lamb chops, shoulder or pork
2 large onions, finely chopped
¼ cup parsley, finely chopped

salt, freshly ground black pepper
8 potatoes, sliced and rinsed in
  cold water
2 cups water

Preheat oven to 375°F. Melt margarine in skillet and when hot sauté chops until brown on both sides; add chopped onions just to lightly brown. Remove chops and onions to shallow oven-serving casserole. Sprinkle meat with parsley, salt, pepper. Drain potato slices and add to chops. Add 2 cups water to skillet over high heat; stir in all the brown meat juices. Pour over casserole; cover and bake until meat is tender, about 1 hour. 8 servings.

American adaptation of hearty peasant bean casserole of France uses West Coast salmon and canned white kidney beans called cannellini for a delicious dish, high in protein. It is good with a fresh spinach salad, and a spicy fruit compote for dessert.

SALMON CASSOULET

1 (16 ounce) can salmon
1 cup elbow macaroni, uncooked
1 tablespoon chopped green pepper
1 clove garlic, minced
¼ cup (½ stick) margarine, melted
⅓ cup flour

2 teaspoons dry mustard
dash hot pepper sauce
2 cups milk
1 cup grated cheese
1 cup canned cannellini beans

Preheat oven to 350°F. Drain salmon; crush bones and leave in for calcium; flake salmon. Cook macaroni; drain. Cook green pepper and garlic in margarine until soft; stir in flour and seasonings. Stir in milk and cook, stirring constantly until thick. Remove from heat and stir in cheese. In greased 2-quart casserole make layers of half the macaroni, cannellini beans, salmon and sauce. Repeat layers. Bake 20 minutes or until hot and bubbly. 6 servings.

Sometimes spelled kibbe and kibby, this is a lamb and cracked wheat shallow meat loaf, cut in diamond shapes for serving. Traditional accompaniment is pita, which is round flat bread, also of the Middle East. Serve with green salad with chopped fresh mint, lemon and oil dressing and chunks of Greek feta cheese.

KIBBI

1½ pounds bulgur (cracked wheat)
2 pounds ground lamb
1 large onion, chopped

2 teaspoons salt
½ teaspoon pepper

Stuffing:

1 pound ground lamb
1 tablespoon margarine
¼ cup pine nuts
1 teaspoon salt

dash each of pepper, cinnamon
½ cup (1 stick) melted margarine
  for top of kibbi
parsley

Preheat oven to 350°F. Rinse wheat in pan of water and drain, then squeeze out all water with hands. Add lamb, onion, salt and pepper and whirl, small amount at a time, in blender a few seconds, until smooth. Spread half the mixture in greased shallow pan, 10 by 15 inches. Start stuffing by sautéing 1 pound lamb in melted margarine over high heat, until lightly browned. Remove from heat and stir in pine nuts, salt, pepper, cinnamon. Spread stuffing evenly over mixture in baking pan. Top with remaining wheat-lamb mixture, patting evenly. Score the kibbi in diamond shapes. Pour stick of melted margarine over top, loosening and lifting edges so margarine may run down into pan. Bake 25 minutes, then run briefly under broiler to brown top. Cut in diamond-shaped pieces and serve with parsley garnish and pita bread. 12 servings.

HOT CHICKEN SALAD

3 cups chopped cooked chicken
2 cups chopped celery
1 (10¾ ounce) can cream of
   mushroom soup, undiluted
1 tablespoon lemon juice

2 tablespoons each, grated onion,
   mayonnaise
2 cups crushed potato chips
½ cup grated sharp Cheddar cheese

Preheat oven to 375°F. Combine all ingredients except potato chips and grated cheese; mix well. Put into greased 2-quart casserole; sprinkle potato chips over top. Bake 20 minutes; sprinkle with cheese and return to oven until cheese melts. 6 servings.

Tian is square, earthenware baking dish of Provence — their shallow casserole. This is a hearty supper dish; follow with cheese (Chevre or goat's milk, perhaps), fresh fruit and red wine.

SPINACH, ZUCCHINI AND EGG TIAN

2 pounds fresh spinach or 2 (10-ounce)
   packages frozen
¼ cup (½ stick) margarine
3 medium-size zucchini, thinly
   sliced
2 onions, thinly sliced

1 to 2 garlic cloves, minced
¼ cup chopped parsley
salt, freshly ground black pepper
4 eggs, slightly beaten
1 cup milk
½ cup grated Parmesan cheese

Preheat oven to 375°F. Wash fresh spinach and remove stems; cook in water that clings to leaves, heating just until wilted. (Thaw frozen spinach.) Fresh or frozen, press spinach in sieve to remove all liquid. Melt margarine in skillet over moderate heat, add zucchini, onion and garlic, cook to soften but not brown. Add spinach and toss together. Add parsley, salt and pepper to taste. Place in greased shallow casserole, 2-quart size. Combine beaten eggs and milk and pour over vegetables. Sprinkle with cheese. Bake until cheese bubbles and eggs are set in center (test with blade of knife) — about 30 minutes. Serve hot or cold. 6 servings.

Not really a casserole, but a unique recipe. Chicken is wrapped in 3-layers of foil, ready to ride safely on the car manifold. After 3-hours of driving the chicken's cooked; moist, tender and delicious!

DEVILED DRUMSTICKS TO GO

1 (3-pound) broiler-fryer chicken, cut-up
½ cup (1 stick) margarine
1 cup fine dry bread crumbs
2 teaspoons each onion powder and curry powder

¾ teaspoon salt
½ teaspoon each dry mustard and garlic powder
½ teaspoon paprika
dash of hot pepper sauce
heavy-duty aluminum foil

Rinse chicken pieces; dry thoroughly; rub with soft margarine and set aside.

In bowl mix bread crumbs, onion and curry powder, salt, dry mustard, garlic powder, paprika and hot pepper sauce. Prepare 3-layers of heavy duty foil, cut large enough to enclose chicken pieces with plenty to fold-over, for tight-fitting package. Dip chicken pieces — rubbed with margarine — into the seasoned bread crumbs. Coat well. Place in single layer on foil; wrap.

Refrigerate until ready to travel.

Roasting on the road: Place foil package of chicken on the exhaust manifold (underneath the hood) of the car. Take off on journey. After 1½-hours of driving stop and turn chicken package (very thick hot-mitts are necessary) to roast the other side. After another 1½ hours of driving it will be chicken dinnertime for 4 hungry travelers.

For another trip:

Wrap a 2-inch thick piece of beef to roast or try hamburger or meat loaf — cooking time and method are the same as for chicken. Results are equally good.

Cheese & Eggs

You may be as innocent as new-laid egg, or as hard-boiled as a picnic egg; have the answer to what came first, the chicken or the egg, and know the moon isn't made of green cheese; but you will be surprised at the variety of ways eggs and cheese can be used on your menus.

In many homes, cheese and eggs are considered "at the ready" ingredients for fast and easy recipes. Served alone or in combination with other foods, they are versatile in their uses for appetizers, main dishes, snacks and desserts, besides being nourishing and easy to digest.

Remember the first principle of protein cookery — especially eggs — LOW temperatures — and you can't fail to produce delicious and tender cheese and egg dishes.

One of the simplest nourishing foods to prepare is the omelet. One thing that keeps its popularity is its variety. Another is the ease of making even elaborate ones.

First, you need some good equipment. For individual omelets get a skillet or pan of medium weight, 6 to 8 inches across top, with sloping sides so that omelet will slide more easily. Coated, non-stick pans are best. For large omelets, electric skillets are a good choice. They come with non-stick surfaces, too.

A good omelet maker has a wide-ranging interest in leftovers; they make excellent omelet fillings. Also he or she soon becomes a good organizer. Omelets are quickly made, so it is necessary to have everything you will use assembled before you start heating the pan. Individual plain omelets cook in a minute; with filling slightly longer, 2 or 3 minutes. Omelets grace the dessert course, too. They are filled with fruits, confections; dusted with sugars or sweetened cocoa; topped with glazes or creams. The variety seems endless. Some are even flamed with brandy.

Having discovered what you can choose to cook, you must now acquire some skill. Practice in private and plan to eat the results even if they look less than decorative. It does not take long to become an expert.

Start first on the basic plain individual omelet. Here is the recipe which serves 2. Uncooked portions can be refrigerated for a while.

4 eggs	1 tablespoon margarine
¼ teaspoon salt	choice of filling optional
¼ cup water	

Put eggs, salt and ¼ cup of water in bowl. Beat briskly with a fork for half a minute, or until yolks and whites are well blended. Heat a 6-inch omelet pan. Put into it 1½ teaspoons margarine. When melted and hot, add ½ of egg mixture. Outer edge of egg should bubble at once and begin to cook. With a spatula push eggs in from side to center of pan. Continue around the outer edge of pan. The uncooked portion flows to bottom of pan. Gently slide pan back and forth over heat to keep from sticking. When set, the omelet is still soft and creamy on top. Cook 1 minute longer to slightly brown bottom. With handle of pan directly in front, put filling (if used) on left side of omelet if you are right-handed; the opposite if left-handed. Use spatula as you would a mixing spoon and turn uncovered side of omelet over filled side. Then with arm and shoulder in an upward movement invert pan over hot serving plate, allowing omelet to drop out.

Repeat cooking process with remaining egg mixture. Use 1½ teaspoons margarine for each omelet. Makes 2 individual omelets. For large omelets, use all margarine and all egg mixture at once. Cook, fill, fold and turn omelet out as directed for individual omelets.

Omelet fillings

SPANISH
---

1 tablespoon minced onion
2 tablespoons minced green pepper
1 tablespoon margarine
1 (8 ounce) can tomato sauce

1 teaspoon sugar
1 teaspoon Worcestershire sauce
dash of hot pepper sauce

Sauté onion and green pepper in margarine a few minutes. Add tomato sauce, sugar, Worcestershire and hot pepper sauce. Simmer, stirring frequently, 5 to 10 minutes, or until fairly thick. 2 servings.

CHICKEN LIVER AND MUSHROOM
---

4 to 5 medium mushrooms
1 tablespoon margarine
1 tablespoon margarine

¼ pound chicken livers
2 green onions
salt and pepper to taste

Slice mushrooms. Sauté in margarine a few minutes; remove mushrooms. Add remaining tablespoon of margarine to skillet, then add chicken livers and sauté with sliced green onions a few minutes on each side. Cut livers in medium pieces, add mushrooms and season to taste with salt and pepper. 2 servings.

ZUCCHINI

2 small zucchini
1 medium onion
1 tablespoon olive oil
1 tomato

¼ cup water
½ teaspoon dried basil leaves
½ cup Mozzarella cheese
Parmesan cheese

Slice zucchini. Sauté with sliced onion in olive oil for a few minutes. Add cut-up tomato, water and dried basil leaves. Cover and simmer a few minutes, or until zucchini is tender and liquid evaporated. Stir in diced Mozzarella cheese. Sprinkle top of folded omelet with grated Parmesan cheese. 2 to 3 servings.

MUSHROOM-SAUSAGE

1 (4 ounce) can Vienna sausages
2 tablespoons margarine
1 (3 ounce) can chopped mushrooms
pinch of cayenne, garlic powder,
    parsley flakes, paprika

1 tablespoon flour
Cheddar cheese

Drain can of Vienna sausages and slice. Melt margarine in saucepan. Add mushrooms, undrained, and sausage. Add cayenne, garlic powder, parsley flakes and paprika. Cook three minutes, then stir in flour. Cook, stirring, until thickened. Sprinkle with shredded Cheddar cheese, add filling, and fold. 2 servings.

SPINACH

creamed spinach   Parmesan cheese

Fill omelet with creamed spinach, sprinkle with grated Parmesan cheese, fold and sprinkle again with cheese.

ITALIAN SAUSAGE

3 or 4 hot or sweet Italian sausages   ½ cup tomato sauce
1 green pepper   ¼ cup water

Slice sausages. Sauté until lightly browned and cooked. Drain off fat and add sliced green pepper, tomato sauce and water to sausage. Simmer, stirring, about 5 minutes. 2 to 3 servings.

ORIENTAL

1 cup drained canned bean sprouts   1 pimiento
3 or 4 water chestnuts (sliced)   2 tablespoons soy sauce
½ cup pork (cooked)

Mix bean sprouts, water chestnuts, finely diced pork, cut-up pimiento and soy sauce. 2 to 3 servings.

2 cups frozen hashed brown potatoes   ½ cup green pepper
1 onion   1 pimiento

Sauté potatoes as directed on label with chopped onion and chopped green pepper. Add cut-up pimiento. 2 servings.

More Filling Suggestions

- Sliced avocado and tomato
- Sliced or diced pepperoni and diced Cheddar cheese
- Flaked tuna, dairy sour cream and sliced black olives
- Diced ham, sliced mushrooms and green onion
- Drained crushed pineapple, cubed cream cheese and crumbled crisp bacon
- Diced salami and cheese and chopped chives
- Fried onions seasoned with salt and sage
- Diced cooked ham and mushrooms and croutons
- Cooked chopped broccoli and diced cheese
- Flaked salmon, chopped water chestnuts and dill
- Cooked cut asparagus, diced ham and grated Swiss cheese
- Curried chicken with chutney to taste
- Any diced cooked meat and canned fried onion rings
- Shredded sharp Cheddar cheese and broken corn chips
- Cooked vermicelli seasoned with minced garlic and mixed with drained minced clams and chopped parsley
- Artichoke hearts and diced cheese
- Cooked frozen Japanese, Italian or Hawaiian vegetables
- Chopped parsley with a pinch each of chervil and tarragon
- Diced cooked chicken livers, mushrooms and water chestnuts; chopped parsley
- Diced cooked shrimps and water chestnuts
- Cooked rice, chopped herbs and pine nuts

DESSERT OMELET — BASIC RECIPE

3 eggs
¼ teaspoon salt

3 tablespoons water
2 tablespoons margarine

With fork, beat eggs, salt and water until blended. Cook in margarine in pan, making one omelette. 2 servings.

Dessert Omelet Fillings

PEANUT

¼ cup salted peanuts
6 tablespoons honey

2 tablespoons orange juice
¼ cup peanut butter (creamy)

Sprinkle omelet with peanuts before folding. Mix honey, orange juice and peanut butter until smooth and blended. Top omelet and serve. 2 servings.

PEACH-CREAM

2 tablespoons dairy sour cream
fresh or canned peaches

toasted nuts

Before folding, spread half the cooked omelet with dairy sour cream. Add peaches. Fold over and turn out on a plate. Spread top with a little sour cream and add a few sliced peaches. Sprinkle with toasted nuts. 2 servings.

MANDARIN ORANGE

sour cream
canned mandarin-orange segments

confectioners' sugar

Fill omelet with sour cream and drained mandarin orange segments. Sprinkle folded omelet with confectioners' sugar. Serves 2.

STRAWBERRY-CREAM

strawberries
sugar

kirsch or Cointreau, if desired
sour cream

Halve strawberries and sweeten with sugar. Add kirsch or Cointreau, if desired. Before folding, spread half the cooked omelet with a little sour cream and top with drained berries. Fold and turn out on plate. Add additional strawberries. 2 servings.

BANANA

sliced bananas
sugar

lemon juice
confectioners' sugar, if desired

Sprinkle bananas with sugar and lemon juice. Fill omelet with the fruit. Fold, sprinkle top with sugar and put under broiler to glaze. Or sprinkle top with confectioners' sugar and omit broiling. 2 servings.

FROSTED

jam, jelly or preferred fruit
1 egg white

2 tablespoons sugar
¼ teaspoon vanilla

Fill omelet with jam, jelly, or preferred fruit. Beat egg white until foamy. Add sugar and vanilla and beat until stiff. Spread on folded omelet and sprinkle with sugar. Broil carefully until golden. 2 servings.

GINGER-CREAM

grated lemon rind to taste
nutmeg to taste
sour cream

ginger (chopped, candied, preserved)

Flavor omelet mixture with grated lemon rind and nutmeg to taste. Fill with sour cream and ginger to taste. 2 servings.

FRUIT-NUT

apple, peach or cherry pie filling | chopped nuts

Variation:

cranberry sauce | slivered almonds

Fill omelet with apple, peach or cherry pie filling and sprinkle folded omelet with chopped nuts. Or fill omelet with cranberry sauce and slivered almonds. 2 servings.

A tempting summer salad meal.

EGG SALAD AND SARDINE FINGERS

Drain 1 can Brisling sardines in oil. Cut crusts from white bread slices then cut slice in three strips. You will need as many strips as you have sardines. Toast bread strips on one side. Spread other side lightly with prepared mustard. Top each with a sardine and broil until brown. Serve with egg salad.

EGG SALAD WITH CHEESE

6 hard-cooked eggs, shelled
   and chopped
1 cup small curd cottage cheese
1 cup chopped celery
2 tablespoons chopped sweet onion
   or chives, or scallions

¼ cup mayonnaise
2 tablespoons chopped parsley
salt and pepper to taste
1 tablespoon sugar
1 tablespoon vinegar
paprika

In a large bowl gently combine all ingredients, except egg, until thoroughly mixed. Gently fold in eggs. Chill. Just before serving sprinkle with paprika. Serve with sardine fingers above. 6 to 8 servings.

For a speedy meal, keep the makings in your pantry, refrigerator or freezer. When needed, you can whip them together like magic. Great for a late supper or surprise lunch.

SWISS HAM ROLLS

8 thin oblong slices cooked ham
8 thin slices Swiss cheese,
   same size
8 cups cooked, canned or
   frozen vegetables

2 tablespoons margarine, melted
salad dressing to taste
parsley or green onions

Arrange thin slice Swiss cheese on top of ham slice. Roll together and fasten with plain toothpick. Repeat until all eight rolls are done. Set aside. Drain cooked or canned vegetables, reserve juices for soup later. Cook frozen vegetables according to directions. Save juices. Choose vegetables such as asparagus, whole green beans, brussels sprouts, artichoke hearts, peas or green lima beans. Pour over them your favorite salad dressing and spoon into an oblong roasting pan. Place pan under preheated broiler until piping hot. Now place broiler grid over vegetables. Arrange ham rolls on broiler grid and brush lightly with melted margarine. Place under broiler just until cheese is melted. Remove ham and vegetables to warm platter. Decorate with parsley or finely chopped green onions. 8 servings.

COTTAGE TIMBALES

1 tablespoon margarine
2 cups Ricotta cheese
2 cups cooked fine noodles
1 tablespoon chopped green pepper

1 teaspoon minced onion
¾ teaspoon salt
¼ cup milk
3 eggs, slightly beaten

Preheat oven to 375°F. Grease 8 custard cups with margarine. Blend remaining ingredients well. Place in custard cups. Set cups in shallow pan of water and bake for 30 to 35 minutes. Unmold and serve with hot spaghetti or pizza sauce. 8 servings.

Here's a nutritious snack that combines some flavors family and friends will like.

CRANBERRY CHEESE BALL

12 oz sharp Cheddar cheese,
  grated
1 (8 oz) package cream cheese
1 tablespoon Worcestershire sauce
½ teaspoon dry mustard

⅓ cup cranberry-orange relish,
  homemade, or processed and
  packed in jars
¾ cup finely chopped
  walnuts or pecans

Grate cheese (Cheddar) as finely as possible; mix with cream cheese until well blended. Stir in Worcestershire sauce and dry mustard. Divide mixture in half. In one half, mix cranberry-orange relish, leave the other half plain. Combine the two halves by swirling the cheeses together. Shape into ball or log and roll in nuts. It can also be thinned with milk and used as a dip by mixing with an electric mixer into a "lumpy" mix. In the blender, the result is a smooth dip. However, the good taste is there either way. 8 to 10 servings.

YOGURT CHEESE

1 quart plain yogurt

½ teaspoon salt

Stir salt into yogurt and pour into sieve lined with double layer of cheesecloth. Sieve is placed over bowl to make it easy to gather up ends of cheesecloth for tying and hanging over faucet of kitchen sink. Let drain overnight. In the morning, empty cheese into dish, cover and refrigerate. Makes 2 cups soft cheese. Serve with breakfast toast, or with salad at lunch. It is best with crisp apples, pears, ripe figs and grapes for dessert.

ITALIAN CHEESE STUFFED SQUASH

2 small or large acorn squash
2 tablespoons margarine

¼ teaspoon salt

Cut acorn squash in half crosswise. Scoop out seeds and slice off bottom so squash rests flat in baking pan. Brush inside with melted margarine and sprinkle with salt.

Cheese Filling

1 tablespoon minced onion
1 tablespoon minced green pepper
1 tablespoon margarine
1 pound Ricotta cheese

2 eggs, slightly beaten
salt and pepper to taste
2 tablespoons margarine, melted

Simmer onion and pepper in margarine until limp and slightly brown. Combine all ingredients thoroughly. Fill squash centers, leaving rounded tops. Brush lightly with melted margarine. Put hot water in pan to ½ inch depth. Bake at 350°F for 35 to 40 minutes. Fill with cheese filling. 4 servings.

AMERICAN INDIAN BEAN DISH

¼ cup salad oil
2 tablespoons cider vinegar
¼ teaspoon tarragon, dried
1 onion, sliced or chopped
salt and pepper to taste

2 tablespoons chopped parsley
1 (16 oz.) can kidney beans
1 loaf whole grain bread
Swiss or Cheddar cheese slices

Combine first six ingredients in a bowl to make dressing; add beans and let marinate, 2 hours or longer. To serve, place bowl on platter, surround with alternate slices of whole grain bread (cut in quarters) and Swiss or Cheddar cheese. Note: Bean Dish ingredients may be whirled in blender to make a delicious dip. 8 servings.

Soft cheese of the Middle east is also called labanee and labneh. Delicious with toasted pita bread, fresh fruit and wine.

Vegetables

The way America cooks fresh vegetables is being turned around — by home gardeners. When the pot bubbles with the first harvest of green beans, tiny beets and tops, or the snow peas you eat pods and all, it's the grower who cares most. And so, to have it their way, gardeners are becoming cooks. Inventive cooks.

Their discovery: Fresh vegetables cooked in minutes while guests watch is an appetite-whetting experience. These First Course Vegetables are eaten crisp-tender, at their flavorful best — well worth the wait!

Cooking time is short: 4 minutes for asparagus to 10 minutes for green beans and carrots — the vegetables that take the longest time. They're cooked in steam, and are the American adaptation of the excellent stir-fry vegetable cuisine of China.

These are steam-cooked in minutes and served as the appetizer or first course at dinner. Guests may fill plates and choose garnishes in kitchen.

The cook thoroughly washes the vegetable then thinly slices it in small pieces, to shorten cooking time. Four cups prepared vegetable is about right for one cooking. Process may be repeated. Cook in a large, 10-inch skillet, margarine, water, salt, pepper.

Have a choice of garnishes ready to offer: bowls of chopped hard-cooked eggs, fried crumbled bacon, chopped scallions, freshly grated Parmesan cheese, crisp croutons, thinly sliced radishes, red and white onions, chopped parsley or watercress; pipkin of hot melted margarine and lemon juice.

Asparagus:

1 pound bunch fresh stalks, snap off stem ends; they'll break at the tender point. Wash thoroughly with cool water, checking for sand. Cut on the diagonal in 2-inch strips. Heat 10-inch skillet over high heat, add 2 tablespoons margarine and when it starts to brown, almost immediately, add asparagus and 3 tablespoons water. Cover and cook over high heat until moisture is gone and vegetable is crisp-tender, about 4 minutes. Add salt, pepper. Serve immediately. Use chopped egg, hot melted margarine and lemon juice as garnish. 3 servings.

Broccoli:

Large bunch makes 4 cups, cut and trimmed. Wash broccoli spears, cut off blossoms and set aside; cut stalks crosswise in 3-inch strips. Peel stalks then cut lengthwise in quarters to make sticks. Cook these stalk-sticks first in 10-inch skillet with 2 tablespoons margarine and ¼ cup water. Cover and cook over high heat 4 minutes. Add blossoms and 3 tablespoons more water; cover and cook 3 minutes more. Serve hot with pipkin of hot melted margarine and fresh lemon juice. 4 servings.

Cabbage:

Shred small head cabbage, about 4 cups. Melt 2 tablespoons margarine in skillet over high heat, add cabbage and ¼ cup water. Cover and cook 5 minutes. Garnish with bacon and Parmesan cheese. 4 servings.

Carrots:

Scrape, wash and thinly slice large bunch carrots to make 4 cupfuls. Add 2 tablespoons margarine to hot skillet, then carrots and ¼ cup water. Cook over high heat 10 minutes, stirring occasionally. Parsley, lemon garnishes. 6 servings.

Cauliflower:

Trim large head then quarter and thinly slice. When 3 tablespoons margarine melts in hot skillet, add cauliflower, then ¼ cup plus 2 tablespoons water; cover and cook 5 minutes. Parmesan cheese and crouton garnish. 6 servings.

Green Beans:

1 pound beans cut on the diagonal in 2-inch lengths. Add to hot skillet with 2 tablespoons margarine, ¼ cup plus 2 tablespoons water; cover and cook 10 minutes. Stirring occasionally. Garnish with bacon and lemon juice. 4 servings.

Green Peas:

4 cups freshly shelled or frozen peas, thawed. Melt 2 tablespoons margarine in hot skillet, add peas, ¼ cup water. Fast cook, covered, 5 minutes for fresh peas, only 2 minutes for frozen. Bacon and onion ring garnish. 6 servings.

Fresh from the garden, these are packed in jars — no need to process. Keep them refrigerated for up to 3 months.

CRISP VEGETABLE PICKLES

4 cups vegetables, thinly sliced:
   medium-size cucumbers, zucchini
   and onions (peel onions only)
2 tablespoons kosher salt
1 cup white vinegar

1 cup sugar
1 clove garlic, minced
1 teaspoon seed of dill, celery
   and/or mustard seed

Thinly slice cucumbers, zucchini and onions then cover with cold water and 2 tablespoons kosher salt. Let stand 2 hours; drain. Pack vegetables in layers in jars; combine vinegar, sugar, garlic and seeds to blend, then pour over vegetables in jars. Cover jars; shake to blend; refrigerate 2 days before using. Makes 2 pints. (Carrots, cauliflower and green beans also may be pickled after cooking to crisp-tender stage then rinsing with cold water.)

Spice, molasses and margarine are the flavor secret.

BEST-EVER BUTTERNUT SQUASH

¾ cup sugar
1 tablespoon flour
¾ teaspoon salt
1 teaspoon each ground nutmeg
   and ginger
2 eggs

3 cups cooked mashed butternut
   squash
1½ cups milk
2 tablespoons light molasses
2 tablespoons margarine, melted

Preheat oven to 350°F. Combine sugar, flour, salt, nutmeg and ginger; beat in eggs. Stir in mashed squash, milk, molasses and margarine. Blend well. Pour into greased 1½ quart casserole. Bake 1 hour and 20 minutes, until firm in the center. 8 servings.

GLAZED CARROTS AND ONIONS

4 carrots, scraped, quartered, cut in
  3 inch sticks
1 (8 ounce) can onions, drained

2 tablespoons sugar
¼ teaspoon ground ginger
2 tablespoons margarine

Steam carrots in small amount of water until crisp-tender, about 10 minutes. Dry carrots and onions on paper. Combine sugar and ginger. Roll vegetables in sugar-ginger covering them thoroughly; then lightly brown in hot margarine in skillet. Toss over high heat until hot and golden. 4 servings.

GLAZED CARROTS

4 cups tender young carrots, cut in
  2 inch sticks
1 cup water
½ teaspoon salt

1½ tablespoons sugar
4 tablespoons (½ stick) margarine

Put carrots, water, salt, sugar and margarine into 10-inch skillet over moderate heat; cover and boil 10 minutes, or less — until crisp-tender. Remove cover and cook over high heat — to evaporate any moisture. Shake pan until carrots are shiny and golden brown. Small white onions may be cooked this way; also white purple-top turnips. Or do the three together — for an interesting first course, garnished with chopped parsley or freshly grated lemon peel. 6 servings.

BAKED BEETS

For fresh, natural flavor slice these and serve as is, hot on dinner plates. Chill some and marinate in vinaigrette sauce for an elegant salad with Boston lettuce, chopped hard-cooked egg.

To do:

Carefully wash beets and cut off all but 2 inches of beet tops and root ends. Wrap in foil and bake in hot oven, 400°F 1 hour or longer, depending on size of beets. Bake alongside of potatoes and/or whole onions in the skins. Great flavor for all three!

Wintertime treat to keep in refrigerator and serve as a different appetizer with cheese and crackers. Colorful buffet relish with chicken and seafood dishes.

PICKLED ORANGE BEETS

¼ cup sugar
½ cup cider vinegar
2 bay leaves

½ cup orange juice
2 cups freshly cooked or canned
   (1 pound) beets, sliced

Simmer sugar, vinegar and bay leaves in saucepan 5 minutes. Stir in orange juice and pour over sliced beets. Cover and chill overnight for flavors to blend. Store up to 2 weeks in refrigerator.

Eggs right from refrigerator are easiest to separate but whites at room temperature beat higher — for lighter souffle. Therefore, separate eggs first in this durable souffle that will "hold" 30 minutes in warm oven, if necessary.

FRESH CORN SOUFFLE

3 eggs
3 ears uncooked sweet corn
   (to make 2 cups juicy kernels)
1 cup grated Cheddar cheese
3 tablespoons packaged biscuit mix
½ teaspoon prepared mustard

pinch of chili powder, or drops
   hot pepper sauce
½ teaspoon salt
1 cup milk
⅛ teaspoon baking powder

Separate eggs; set aside. Cut kernels from cob, using sharp blade then back of blade to scrape off some of the pulp and juice. Mix corn with cheese. Preheat oven to 350°F and place oven rack somewhat low for baking. Combine biscuit mix, mustard, chili powder and salt in a saucepan and very gradually stir in milk. Place over moderate heat and when hot, stir in cheese and corn mixture. Add a little of this hot sauce to egg yolks, stirring constantly. Return all to saucepan, stir until hot, then remove from heat. Let rest. Add baking powder to egg whites and beat to soft peaks; gently fold into corn mixture. Pour into ungreased 1½ quart casserole. Place in larger pan of warm water then onto oven rack to bake for 55 minutes. Test with point of knife inserted in center of souffle — it should come out clean. 4 servings.

SWEDISH BEET APPLE SALAD

1 pound jar fancy sliced beets
2 tablespoons dry minced onion
1 large or 2 small apples, cored and
    sliced with peel on

⅔ cup cider vinegar
1 tablespoon sugar
½ teaspoon salt
¼ teaspoon pepper

Drain beets, reserving juice. Measure ⅓ cup beet juice and combine with ⅔ cup vinegar, sugar, salt, and pepper. Pour over beets and sliced apples. Let stand several hours to pickle.

Store in refrigerator to garnish sandwiches, salad plates.

FRESH CUCUMBER PICKLE

4 large cucumbers, peeled, sliced
    wafer-thin
2 tablespoons salt
2 cups cider vinegar

1¼ cups sugar
½ teaspoon black pepper
2 tablespoons minced fresh parsley

Spread cucumber slices over a couple plates, sprinkle with salt and let stand at room temperature 1 hour. Drain slices on paper towels, pressing with hands. Combine all other ingredients in pan, heat to boiling then let cool. Pour cool marinade over cucumber slices in glass dish. Let stand in room 2 hours or over night in refrigerator, then chill and drain before serving. 8 servings.

Amazingly good with roast chicken or turkey, pork or beef.

SAUTÉED ONION SLICES

½ cup (1 stick) margarine
4 large onions, peeled and sliced
    ½ inch thick

½ teaspoon salt
½ teaspoon nutmeg
½ cup grated Parmesan cheese

Melt margarine in 10 inch skillet over low heat; add onions, cover and cook about 30 minutes, until tender. Add salt and nutmeg then taste. Serve in heated dish with Parmesan cheese sprinkled over the top. 8 servings.

CUCUMBERS IN YOGURT

1 large cucumber, peeled
2 tablespoons mayonnaise
½ cup yogurt
2 tablespoons lemon juice

½ teaspoon sugar
⅛ teaspoon dry mustard
salt and pepper to taste
paprika, fresh parsley and dill

Slice a large cucumber thinly. Arrange on platter. Combine remaining ingredients and pour over cucumber. Sprinkle with paprika, parsley and dill, snipped. 2 to 4 servings.

GOLDEN GOODNESS SALAD BOWL

salad greens
2 cups coarsely grated, raw carrot
4 large slices pineapple

mayonnaise, walnuts and nutmeg,
    as desired

Shred salad greens and spread over flat platter. Sprinkle carrots over greens in 4 mounds. Top each mound with pineapple slice. Spread mayonnaise over pineapple. Sprinkle with walnut pieces. Grate fresh nutmeg all over. 4 servings.

Wrapped in foil, heated bubbling hot in oven or on grill; it's your choice!

TANGY GREEN BEANS

2 (10 ounce) packages frozen
    green beans

1 onion, thinly sliced
½ cup bottled Italian dressing

Place frozen beans atop large, double-thick square of foil. Add onion rings and turn up sides of foil. Pour Italian dressing over beans. Fold top of foil tightly. Place in 350°F oven or on hot grill for 30 minutes. Serve hot. 6 servings.

It's a meal with crusty bread, cheese and fruit to follow. Pour a young Beaujolais or your favorite Zinfandel wine.

HEARTY HOT POTATO SALAD

4 large potatoes
1 large red onion, finely chopped
8 slices bologna, diced
1 red apple, cored and diced
2 stalks celery, thinly sliced
1 (2-ounce) can anchovy fillets,
   drained and chopped

4 slices bacon, diced
¼ cup vinegar
1 tablespoon sugar
½ teaspoon each salt,
   Worcestershire sauce
few drops hot pepper sauce
1 egg yolk

Boil potatoes in skins until tender; drain and set aside to keep warm. In salad bowl mix onion, bologna, apple, celery, anchovy fillets and toss; peel and dice potatoes and add. In skillet over moderate heat cook bacon until crisp; lift out bacon pieces and add to potatoes. Measure out 3 tablespoons of the bacon fat — discard the rest. Beat with fork the vinegar, sugar, salt, Worcestershire (hot pepper sauce) and egg yolk; combine with bacon fat and heat, stirring until sauce is hot and thickened. Pour this hot sauce over potatoes; toss and serve. 8 servings.

POTATOES ANNA

8 medium-size baking potatoes
½ cup (1 stick) margarine, softened

salt to taste

Preheat oven to 400°F. Pare and thinly slice potatoes. Generously grease bottom and sides of shallow baking dish. Arrange potato slices in overlapping layers to completely cover bottom of dish. Spread each layer with soft margarine and sprinkle with salt; repeat until all potatoes are used. Spread remaining margarine over top. Bake in hot oven until potatoes are soft in the center, crisp at the edges and brown on the bottom. During cooking cover top with foil if potatoes are browning too fast. Takes 45 minutes to 1 hour. To serve, invert potatoes onto heated platter. 8 servings.

Parboiling potatoes helps keep cream sauce from curdling, for more attractive servings. Delicious dish with cold meat — especially with chicken or turkey the second day.

SCALLOPED POTATOES

3 pounds potatoes (about 8)
4 onions, thinly sliced
4 tablespoons flour
1½ teaspoons salt

½ teaspoon freshly ground
   black pepper
2 cups milk, hot
2 tablespoons margarine

Preheat oven to 375°F. Pare and thinly slice potatoes, parboil in boiling salted water almost to cover 3 minutes; drain. Layer potatoes and onions in a greased 2½ quart baking dish, sprinkling layers with flour, salt, pepper. Pour hot milk over potatoes, dot with margarine. Cover and bake 45 minutes. Uncover and bake 15 minutes longer, until potatoes are tender and top is golden. 8 servings.

Oven-baked alongside roast chicken, add a handful of cranberries for color, chopped nuts for texture.

SWEET POTATOES AND APPLES

4 medium-size sweet potatoes
4 large apples
¾ cup light brown sugar, packed
½ teaspoon salt

½ teaspoon cinnamon
1 tablespoon lemon juice
4 tablespoons (½ stick) margarine
½ cup warm water

Boil potatoes then peel and slice 1-inch thick. Pare and core apples and slice into ½-inch rings. In greased baking dish arrange potatoes and apples in layers; sprinkle with brown sugar, salt, cinnamon and lemon juice. Dot with margarine. Add water and cover. Bake at 375°F 35 minutes; remove cover and bake another 10 minutes. 6 servings.

No need to peel, just scrub with stiff brush and cold water. Cut in half, drop into pan with 2-inches boiling salted water. Boil until fork-tender, about 10 minutes. Mash 2 or 3 anchovies with ½ stick (¼ cup) soft margarine for each pound potatoes. Drain potatoes; toss with anchovy-margarine in pan. Serve steaming hot, with dusting of chopped parsley if you like. 4 servings.

Medley of vegetables that's more delicious made ahead and reheated or served cold. An appetizer with crusty bread and wine, or as vegetable on the dinner plate. (Ratatouille sounds like rata-too-ee)

RATATOUILLE

½ cup (1 stick) margarine, divided
2 onions, sliced
3 cloves garlic, minced
1 medium-size eggplant, in
   ½-inch cubes
flour

2 medium-size zucchini, thickly sliced
4 green or red peppers, cut in strips
1½ teaspoons salt
1 tablespoon chopped fresh basil, or
   1 teaspoon dried
8 firm-ripe tomatoes, in chunks

Heat half the margarine in a large skillet over high heat; add onions and garlic and cook, stirring to soften — not brown. In another pan heat rest of margarine over high heat; add eggplant cubes lightly coated with flour. Saute few minutes, until golden. Arrange eggplant and pan drippings in layer over onions; add zucchini, pepper strips, seasonings and tomatoes. Cover pan and cook over moderate heat about 30 minutes. Vegetables will be firm-tender with juice for spooning onto plates. If too much juice, remove tender vegetables and rapidly boil juice to reduce and thicken, then pour over vegetables to serve hot, or store and serve later — hot or cold. Appetizer garnish could be thin slice of tomato and chopped parsley or fresh basil. 10 servings.

TOMATOES STUFFED WITH SPINACH

6 medium-size tomatoes
4 strips bacon, fried and crumbled
1 (10 ounce) package frozen chopped
  spinach
¾ cup soft breadcrumbs, chopped
  fine in blender

salt, pepper, nutmeg
3 tablespoons margarine, melted
Parmesan cheese, freshly grated

Not necessary to peel tomatoes. Cut thin slice off top of each and scoop out center pulp (no need to save). Turn tomatoes upside down to drain. Cook bacon. Thaw spinach, over heat if you like. Drain spinach and press out liquid. Combine with breadcrumbs, seasonings to taste; add crumbled bacon. Loosely stuff tomatoes and place in greased shallow baking pan — or pie plate. Spoon melted margarine over tops of tomatoes and refrigerate. Bake uncovered in 400°F oven 10 minutes or place low under broiler until tomatoes and spinach are hot. Serve with sprinkling of freshly grated Parmesan cheese. 6 servings.

This green squash can hide under leaves of the same color, grow big and mature — zucchini grandfathers. Slice these in flat strips, dip in batter and pan fry. Good flavor.

CRUSTY ZUCCHINI GRANDFATHERS

1 cup grated Parmesan cheese
2 eggs
2 tablespoons flour
1 teaspoon salt
½ teaspoon pepper
1 clove garlic, minced

2 tablespoons chopped parsley
¼ cup milk
2 large zucchini, 8 to 10 inches long
flour for dusting
½ cup (1 stick) margarine

Make batter first by beating together until smooth the cheese, eggs, flour, salt, pepper, garlic, parsley and milk. Refrigerate 15 minutes or longer before using. Meanwhile slice zucchinis crosswise in half, then in flat strips 3-inches long, 1 inch-wide and ¼-inch thick. Using 10-inch skillet, heat margarine over moderate heat. With fork or fingers, dip each zucchini slice into batter to thickly coat; drop into bubbling margarine and cook, a few at a time, until golden on both sides. Drain on paper towels and keep warm. Serve hot with more Parmesan cheese if you like. 6 servings.

Recipe of public television's Home Gardener. He says this is the ONLY way to cook zucchini.

TWO-MINUTE ZUCCHINI

3 small zucchini
2 tablespoons margarine

salt
pepper

Wash zucchini and cut-off stem and blossom ends. Using hand grater, coarsely grate zucchini into plate placed underneath grater. Heat 10-inch skillet over high heat; add margarine and when it bubbles add zucchini, tossing lightly with fork. Cover for a very few seconds if you like, but 2 minutes cooking is all it takes to heat thoroughly. Add salt and pepper to taste. Serve hot vegetable that's light as a souffle with garden-fresh flavor. 4 servings.

RAW MUSHROOM, RADISH, BOSTON LETTUCE SALAD

12 large mushrooms
juice of 2 lemons
12 red radishes
1 head Boston lettuce, rinsed and
   chilled
1 teaspoon salt

½ teaspoon freshly ground
   black pepper
2 tablespoons chopped chives
½ cup celery or fennel,
   finely chopped
¼ cup salad oil

Wash mushrooms and cut off dry stem end; slice mushrooms very thin. Immediately pour lemon juice over mushrooms, coating them well. Slice radishes; tear lettuce into large pieces and place in salad bowl with mushrooms. Combine salt, pepper, chives, celery and salad oil; pour over salad and mix well. Serve in chilled salad bowls. 6 servings.

There are many recipes for this American-original, but this one MUST be made at the last minute — while guests watch. Good theatre!

CAESAR SALAD WITH DRAMA

salt, garlic clove
3 heads romaine, endive, or
   escarole — not lettuce
5 anchovy fillets, mashed
¼ cup salad oil
few drops Worcestershire sauce
freshly ground black pepper

¼ cup grated Parmesan cheese
1 egg, simmered 1 minute in shell
juice of 2 lemons
1 cup hot, freshly made croutons
   (sauteed in margarine with
   garlic clove)

Using hands, rub salad bowl with salt then garlic clove (what's left of garlic may be minced and added to ¼ cup salad oil). Break crisp romaine, endive, and/or escarole into bite-size pieces and toss in salad bowl. In small bowl, mix anchovy paste with salad oil, Worcestershire, freshly ground pepper and Parmesan cheese. Break egg into bowl, add lemon juice and beat with fork. Pour over salad greens and toss. Serve in chilled salad bowls with hot croutons added. 8 servings.

Prepare vegetables the night before, then chill until crackling-crisp. In fall and winter, garnish bowl with freshly sliced red apples.

CELERY-CARROT COLESLAW

4 cups finely shredded cabbage
1 cup thinly sliced celery, cut on
   the diagonal
1 cup shredded carrot
½ cup thinly sliced onion, in
   half-circles

¼ cup chopped parsley
½ cup each mayonnaise and
   sour cream
salt, sugar, hot pepper sauce

Put shredded cabbage into icy-cold water to chill while preparing other vegetables. Thoroughly drain cabbage then combine with celery, carrot, onion and parsley. Package and chill. When ready to serve, drain any moisture from vegetables then toss with mayonnaise and sour cream; add salt, sugar and hot pepper sauce to taste. 8 servings.

BROILED TOMATOES ALL-YEAR

During garden season, cut medium-size tomatoes in half and sprinkle tops with margarine creamed with salt, freshly ground pepper, pinch of sugar, sprinkling of basil and a little thyme, herbs fresh or dried. Prepare ahead and let stand at room temperature. Broil, bake or grill at high heat about 10 minutes, until topping bubbles and is lightly browned.

In Winter, use canned plum tomatoes that have been well drained of their juice. Minced onion or garlic may be added.

FRESH MUSHROOM SALAD

½ pound mushrooms, sliced through
   stems
1 cup salad oil
½ cup vinegar
½ teaspoon tarragon leaves

¼ teaspoon ground nutmeg
½ teaspoon salt
1 head each romaine and
   Boston lettuce

Slice washed mushrooms into deep bowl; add oil, vinegar, tarragon, nutmeg, salt and mix; let stand at room temperature 1 hour, stirring occasionally. Wash salad greens and break in bite-size pieces. Mix lightly with mushrooms and dressing in bowl. Serve. 8 servings.

SWEET-SOUR BEAN SALAD

2 pounds fresh green beans
1½ teaspoons salt
¼ cup (½ stick) margarine
1 onion sliced

½ cup cider vinegar
¼ cup water
½ cup sugar
romaine or escarole spears

Slice beans on the diagonal in 1-inch slices. Steam in ½ cup water about 10 minutes, until crisp-tender and bright green. Drain. While hot, add salt, margarine, and onion. Cool. Combine vinegar, water and sugar and pour over beans. Chill. Serve on crisp greens on chilled salad plates. Garnish with a bit of red if you like: radishes, cherry tomatoes, cooked beets. 8 servings.

GREEN GODDESS SALAD

3 heads Boston lettuce
2 tablespoons anchovy fillets, minced
   to paste
1 cup mayonnaise
2 tablespoons fresh lemon juice
½ cup sour cream

½ cup cider vinegar
¼ cup each chopped onion, minced
   parsley
few leaves fresh tarragon or ¼
   teaspoon dried

Rinse lettuce and break in bite-size pieces; wrap and chill 1 hour or longer. Stir anchovy paste into mayonnaise. Add lemon juice to sour cream and mix well. Combine the two with vinegar, chopped onion, parsley, and tarragon. Chill this dressing. To serve, pour over salad greens and toss. 12 servings.

ROMAINE WITH MUSTARD DRESSING

1 bunch romaine
2 tablespoons salad oil
1 tablespoon prepared spicy mustard
1 tablespoon cider vinegar

½ teaspoon salt
freshly ground black pepper
2 hard-cooked eggs, finely chopped

Wash romaine leaves; break in bite-size pieces; wrap and chill 1 hour or longer. In chilled salad bowl mix together the oil, mustard, vinegar, salt, pepper and chopped eggs. Add the thoroughly drained and chilled romaine. Toss to coat greens. Serve. 8 servings.

Fruit

When planning a party, special dinner, picnic or barbecue, think first of fruit. Fruit combined with flowers for the centerpiece: fresh pears, red apples, figs, lemons, papayas from Hawaii, new kiwi fruit, ripe plums, red ripe strawberries.

Try a tart and tangy salad to open dinner — crisp spears of romaine on chilled plates with grapefruit, orange and avocado or melon. Spoon on a light dressing of equal parts of lemon juice and honey; some toasted sesame seeds.

Another time serve fruit with the entree; replacing one of the vegetables served with meat, fish or poultry. Try peaches or apricots and green beans with beef — applesauce, steamed carrots and broccoli with pork or chicken. Make seafood special by adding sauteed bananas — our 12 month fruit.

For dessert, take fruit from the centerpiece and add icy cold grapes, cheese at room temperature: ripe and runny brie, a chunk of blue cheese, some fresh chevre cheese (goat's milk).

Serve as fruit cup, buffet dish, dessert or table centerpiece in bowl of ice with flowers circling melon.

MELON SURPRISE

1 large canteloupe, cranshaw,
  honeydew or Persian melon
peaches, pears in season
grapes, pineapple
berries in season

lemon juice
ground cardamom, nutmeg
white or rosé wine
sugar and salt, to taste

Cut generous slice off top of melon; remove seeds, then scoop out melon either making balls or chopping pieces. Toss these with other prepared fruits, lemon juice, dash of spice and wine. Taste and add just a dash of sugar and/or salt, but only if necessary. Heap into melon shell; cover with reserved slice from top and refrigerate to chill thoroughly. Additional whole strawberries, pineapple cubes on picks, sprigs of fresh mint may be used to surround and garnish whole melon when served atop bowl of ice. 6 to 12 servings, depending on size of melon and other fruits added.

As a change from vegetables with ham, chicken or lamb dinner; a do-ahead for cookouts, picnics, Sunday brunches.

WARM CURRIED FRUIT

1 (16 ounce) can peach or apricot
  halves, drained
1 (16 ounce) can pear halves, drained
1 (16 ounce) can pineapple slices,
  drained

¼ cup (½ stick) margarine
¾ cup light brown sugar, packed
1 to 3 teaspoons curry powder
1 cup blanched almonds, slivered

Drain fruit spread out over paper towels; arrange in layers in 1½ quart shallow baking dish; plan top layer for pretty effect. Melt margarine in saucepan with brown sugar, curry powder and nuts. Spoon over fruit. Bake in slow, 325°F oven 1 hour. Serve hot or warm. Make ahead and reheat if you like. Serve with a dollop of sour cream, if desired. 8 servings.

HOLIDAY FRUIT RING CENTERPIECE

Choose fruits in season: grapes, kumquats, dates, figs, cranberries attractively arranged together, smallest lemons, oranges and tangerines, rosy lady apples of winter.

Dip each piece of fruit into egg whites — beaten only until frothy — then roll in granulated sugar. Let dry. Arrange colorfully as fruit ring on serving platter. An interesting gift, tied with a handsome red or green velvet ribbon.

New-day apple pie — without the pastry. Extra flavor from two-nut combination: walnuts AND pecans.

ELEGANT APPLE CRISP

8 good size apples
1½ cups light brown sugar, packed
1 cup unsifted flour
¼ teaspoon salt

½ cup each walnuts and pecans, chopped
½ cup (1 stick) margarine

Preheat oven to 350°F. Peel, core and thinly slice apples; place in shallow 2 quart baking dish. Spread with ½ the brown sugar. Combine remaining sugar, flour, salt and nuts; using fingers rub margarine into mixture until it crumbles. Spread over apples, pressing down around edges so topping completely covers apples. Bake in oven 1 hour. Serve warm with sour cream. 8 servings.

KIWI FRUIT

Newcomer to supermarkets is the kiwi from New Zealand, now grown in California as well. This egg-shaped fruit has a fuzzy brown skin on the outside, green interior and flavor that's a delicious blend of pineapple, papaya, strawberry and banana. One peeled, crosswise slice of this exotic fruit atop a salad or dessert makes a conversation piece. And good eating!

"Ananas au Grand Marnier" to the French, who serve this with extra dry Champagne.

FRESH PINEAPPLE WITH LIQUEUR
---

1 ripe pineapple   Grand Marnier liqueur

Keep pineapple at room temperature until it exudes a sweetness, when held to the nose. Retaining spike on top, cut pineapple lengthwise in 4 portions; using a flexible knife remove fruit from shells. Cut fruit in cubes, removing core. Marinate fruit in several ounces of Grand Marnier. To serve, heap shells with fruit and you might garnish with a fresh flower — as in Honolulu. 4 servings.

Chutney means many things to different countries, and recipes for it are used in different ways. Here is a prize winner. Easy to make. Keeps months in covered jar in refrigerator. The cooking quantity may be tripled. Use with cold meats, cheeses, baked hams, bland fruits such as bananas, toasted muffins or anything else your imagination prompts.

WEST INDIAN APPLE CHUTNEY

2½ cups (one 1 pound 4 ounce   ½ teaspoon salt
   can) sliced apples, undrained   1 teaspoon each of ground
1 cup raisins   ginger and dry mustard
¾ cup unsulphured molasses   1 tablespoon curry powder
½ cup cider vinegar

Mix all ingredients in saucepan. Bring to boil, stirring to blend ingredients. Simmer, uncovered, over low heat for 15 minutes, stirring occasionally. Makes 3 cups.

SPICED CRANBERRY-ORANGE DESSERT

3 oranges
2 cups sugar
1 cup water
4 inches cinnamon stick

6 whole cloves
4 cups fresh cranberries
 (1 pound bag)

Peel oranges, cut in ½-inch slices, then quarter each slice. Boil sugar, water and spices together 5 minutes; add cranberries, cook 5 minutes, until skins just start to pop. Add orange pieces and simmer another 2 minutes. Cool, then chill. Serve in chilled sherbet glasses with a scoop of lemon sherbet placed on top of each serving if desired. 12 servings.

BANANAS FOSTER

¼ cup (½ stick) margarine
½ cup light brown sugar, packed
4 firm-ripe bananas, peeled and
 halved lengthwise

dash cinnamon
¼ cup banana liqueur
½ cup white rum
1 pint vanilla ice cream

Melt margarine and brown sugar in flat pan of chafing dish, or use skillet. Add bananas and saute, basting with sauce, until tender. Sprinkle with cinnamon. Pour banana liqueur and warm rum over all, then flame. Baste with warm liquid until flame burns out. Serve immediately over ice cream. 4 to 6 servings.

Easy to make relish keeps 3 weeks in refrigerator. Serve with pork, chicken and seafood. Serve with sandwiches and other snack meals.

CARDAMOM PEACH PICKLE

2 (29 ounce) cans peach halves
1 whole orange, chopped
1 cup cider vinegar

1 cup sugar
1 teaspoon ground cardomom

Pour peach syrup into saucepan, add finely chopped orange, vinegar, sugar and cardomom. Simmer, covered, 15 minutes. Place peach halves in covered jar; fill with hot syrup. Cover, cool 1 hour then refrigerate. Makes 3 pint jars.

Another time, use canned drained pears or pineapple chunks with this gingerbread. Fill the house with the spicy-good fragrance of home baking.

UPSIDE DOWN APPLE GINGERBREAD

¼ cup (½ stick) margarine
½ cup brown sugar, packed
1 teaspoon cinnamon

3 apples peeled and cored
1 (14½ ounce) package
   gingerbread mix

Melt margarine in bottom of 9-inch square baking pan. Combine brown sugar and cinnamon; sprinkle over margarine. Cut apples into rings and arrange in pan over margarine mixture. Prepare gingerbread according to package directions; pour batter over apple slices. Bake as gingerbread package directs. Invert onto serving plate. Serve warm with ice cream. Makes 8 servings.

Traditional in the South for Christmas dinner menu, this is the authentic recipe. Make ahead and refrigerate for flavors to blend.

AMBROSIA

---

6 large sweet juicy oranges
4 ripe bananas
1 red apple, diced

1 (3½ ounce) can flaked coconut
dash salt

Cut oranges over bowl, to retain juice; pare off peel as for an apple then remove all white membrane. Remove orange sections by pushing knife blade between fruit and membrane. Peel bananas and slice over orange sections in bowl. Dice apple and toss with oranges — to keep from discoloring. Add coconut and salt. Toss lightly and add more coconut, if wanted. Chopped pecans may be added. Chill for serving. 8 servings.

FRESH APPLE APPLESAUCE

½ cup water
¼ cup sugar, or to taste
¼ teaspoon salt

1 teaspoon ascorbic acid (to prevent
darkening of raw fruit)
1 pound tart apples (2 or 3)

In blender combine water, sugar, salt and ascorbic acid (sold with freezer supplier; some drugstores). Peel and core apples and slice into blender. Run blender at high speed 30 seconds — or less. 6 servings.

As served in Madrid and all over Spain; superb flavor blend to start a meal or finish it.

STRAWBERRY-ORANGE FRIO

1 pint ripe strawberries
1 cup orange juice

fresh mint

Rinse berries, then hull and heap in sherbet glasses. Cover with freshly squeezed orange juice. Add a sprig of mint.

DOROTHY'S HOMEMADE CHUTNEY

2 (9 ounce) packages concentrated
mincemeat, crumbled
1 (8 ounce) package pitted dates,
chopped
1 (8 ounce) package dried apricots,
chopped

1 chopped onion
1 clove garlic, minced
2 cups cider vinegar
1 cup sugar

Combine all ingredients; add 1 cup water then heat to boiling; reduce heat and simmer 10 minutes, stirring constantly. Spoon into covered jars; cool then refrigerate. Makes 3 pints.

With frozen puff pastry shells from the freezer and this step-by-step recipe you're ready to make and serve a Tarte aux Fruits — the real thing!

EASY FRENCH FRUIT TART

2 (10-ounce) packages frozen puff pastry shells

Let pastry shells thaw at room temperature one hour. They should feel cool to the touch, when they're ready.

Filling — Creme Patisserie

½ cup sugar
6 tablespoons cornstarch
4 egg yolks

3 cups milk
3 teaspoons vanilla

Mix sugar and cornstarch in top of double boiler or use heatproof bowl set into larger saucepan with simmering water in the bottom. (Bowl should be above the water, not touching it). Beat egg yolks then add milk and stir into sugar and cornstarch. Place over simmering water, stirring constantly until mixture thickens, about 10 minutes. Cook, without stirring, about 5 minutes longer. Pour into a cool bowl and stir in vanilla. Chill.

Pastry Shell

Place 6 thawed shells atop each other and press together gently. On a light floured board roll out to an oblong 11 by 5 inches; trim edges with a sharp knife. Place on cookie sheet, and chill. Using remaining 6 shells, roll out another oblong 11 by 5 inches. Measure in ¾-inch from all edges and cut out center pastry, using a sharp knife. This is a pastry frame.

Take chilled oblong from refrigerator, brush with water and set pastry frame on top. Press together to seal. Prick center of bottom layer with fork. Chill 30 minutes. Preheat oven to 450°F. (Pastry removed from second oblong may be chilled then brushed with sugar and nuts and baked separately.) Take pastry case from refrigerator, place on center rack in oven and close door. Immediately reduce heat to 400 degrees; bake 20 to 25 minutes, until puffed and rich gold color. Remove to wire rack to cool. Cut out puffed center flakes of pastry to form as deep a shell as possible.

Fruit for Topping

12 whole strawberries, washed
  and hulled
12 green grapes, clean and dry

2 navel oranges, peeled and
  sectioned
¼ cup light corn syrup

To Assemble Tart

Spoon cooled filling into pastry shell; spread to smooth top. Arrange a long row of strawberries along one side; grapes in a single row along the opposite side; slightly mound orange sections to fill the center in orderly fashion. Brush fruit lightly with corn syrup and chill until serving time. 8 servings.

Superb wintertime dessert served with wine. And the glistening fruit in warm sauce makes a fine relish for a ham or pork buffet.

SPICY FRUIT COMPOTE

---

1 (29-ounce) can each peach and
  pear halves
1 (20-ounce) can sliced pineapple
1 (17-ounce) can sliced apples or
  Kadota figs

½ cup light brown sugar, packed
¼ cup (½ stick) margarine
1 teaspoon each ginger and
  curry powder
¼ teaspoon salt

Thoroughly drain fruits; save all syrup to use in gelatin desserts, meat glazes etc.

In small saucepan combine brown sugar, margarine, ginger, curry powder and salt. Heat and stir to boiling; remove from heat.

Arrange fruits attractively, round side up for peaches and pears; pour and spoon on margarine-brown sugar glaze, coating top well. Bake in 350°F oven 30 minutes, basting with syrup. Serve warm. 6 servings.

Serve warm with roast ham or save for dessert and add a sprinkling of nuts and raisins.

HONEY BAKED APPLES

6 large apples
6 tablespoons honey

½ cup orange juice
sugar, nutmeg

Preheat oven to 400°F. Choose Rome Beauties or Cortland apples, if available; these varieties hold their shape well — do not collapse — during baking. Core apple, being careful not to cut all the way through the bottom. Peel ½ the way down the top-stem end. Combine honey and orange juice and use to fill apples. Set in deep baking dish. Pour ½ inch water in bottom of pan. Bake 45 to 60 minutes, until apples are tender. Sprinkle tops with a little sugar and nutmeg; run under broiler to glaze. 6 servings.

Of sherbet consistency, this is almost a daiquiri, and most refreshing. Use less ice, serve in tulip glasses with straws and it's a beverage. Versatile invention!

FROSTED PINEAPPLE FROTH

2 jiggers light rum, chilled
3 slices fresh pineapple, cut fine

1 tablespoon sugar
3 cups cracked ice

While chilling rum, also chill blender container, for everything has to be COLD. Put everything, including ice, into chilled blender. Blend to sherbet consistency. Heap into chilled sherbet dishes. Add sprig of mint (more mint may be blended with rum and all if you like.) 2 servings.

Bread & Rolls

Whatever the meal — a home-baked loaf, pan of lofty popovers from the oven, a big bowlful of soft-and-salty pretzels twisted and shaped your way — any of these makes a meal a banquet. There's no haute(ier) cuisine than bread baked at home!

When time is short there's quick bread, leavened with baking powder and/or soda. Irish soda bread, biscuits and banana bread are a few. There are several hundred more . . . shared by every country in the world.

It takes four hours or longer to make and bake yeast bread. Success starts with sprinkling dry yeast from the package into very warm water (105 to 115 degrees on the cooking thermometer) then giving it a spoonful of sugar to feed on. Soon there will be foam and bubbles as the microscopic yeast plants begin to grow and grow . . . The steadier their growth the lighter the finished loaf.

1 package active dry yeast (2 packages will reduce the time about half)
¼ cup very warm water (105 to 115 degrees)
pinch of sugar

2 cups milk, scalded
2 teaspoons salt
2 tablespoons sugar
2 tablespoons margarine
6 cups flour, about

Sprinkle dry yeast over warm water in cup, add a pinch of sugar for yeast to feed and grow on; set aside for 5 minutes. Pour hot milk into large mixing bowl with salt, sugar ane margarine. When milk mixture is lukewarm (a drop on the wrist should feel warm — not hot) add 3 cups of the flour and beat 3 minutes, using electric beater. Use spoon to stir in remaining 3 cups of flour. Stir until dough forms a ball. Turn onto lightly floured board and cover with bowl for 20 minutes.

Knead dough about 10 minutes, adding flour if necessary, until it looks smooth and elastic. Roll dough around in greased bowl, cover lightly and let rise in warm place until double in bulk. Turn dough onto lightly floured board and knead ever so lightly for only 30 seconds. Divide dough in half and use fingers to press dough into 9-inch squares. (2 of them.) Shape by rolling up jelly roll fashion. Place in two well-greased 9-inch loaf pans. Cover lightly and let rise in warm place until double in bulk. Bake on rack in center of 375°F oven 45 to 50 minutes. Remove from pans. Makes 2 loaves.

Trick: for VERY crusty rolls, place shallow pan of boiling water on bottom of oven just before baking. Steam hardens crust.

CRUSTY DINNER ROLLS

1¼ cups warm (105 to 115
   degrees) water
3 tablespoons margarine
1 teaspoon salt

1 tablespoon sugar
1 package active dry yeast
4 to 4½ cups unbleached flour
2 egg whites, beaten

In large mixing bowl (rinsed with hot water to heat bowl then dried) place the warm water, margarine, salt, sugar and dry yeast from package. Add 1 cup of the flour and beat at low speed — with electric beater — 2 minutes. Beat egg whites to soft peaks then stir in by hand. Continue to stir by hand, adding 3 cups flour (no more unless necessary), to make a stiff dough.

Place ball of dough onto LIGHTLY floured board and knead 8 to 10 minutes, adding a bit more flour if dough sticks.

Grease bowl then roll dough in it (to prevent dry top); cover and let rise in warm place until double in bulk. Punch down, remove from bowl and cut in 12 pieces. Roll each piece in a ball or pillow-shape and place on greased cookie sheets about 2½-inches apart. Cover lightly and let rise in warm place until double in bulk. Brush with water and bake in 400°F oven 15 minutes. One dozen rolls.

The texture and slightly sour tang of this bread make it different, as any San Franciscan will tell you. This sourdough starter is the safe one; it contains yeast. Make it at least 4 days ahead of time, to be sure it's alive with the aroma of sourdough. Always bring starter to room temperature before using.

Sourdough Starter

1 package active dry yeast
2 cups warm water (105 to
   114 degrees)

2 cups unbleached flour

Sprinkle yeast over water; set aside 5 minutes. Gradually add flour, beating with electric beater at medium speed. When mixture is smooth, cover lightly in warm place (85 degrees) until bubbles come to the top, about 24 hours. (No bubbles? Yeast is dead so toss out starter and begin again with more yeast.)

Thoroughly stir the bubbly starter; cover. Let stand in warm place 2 days or until foamy. Stir well and sniff the good sourdough aroma, then remove 1 cupful for whole wheat bread. Pour rest of starter into tightly covered container and store in refrigerator. Once a week give starter 1 teaspoon sugar for yeast to feed on. To replenish starter, add 1 cup each flour and warm water then let stand in warm place until bubbles are renewed. Always stir starter to mix well before using; measure out 1 cupful for recipe and give it time to come to room temperature before blending with other ingredients. Return the jar of starter to refrigerator until next used.

1½ cups hot water
½ cup (1 stick) margarine
1 package active dry yeast
Pinch of sugar
1 egg
½ cup sugar

½ teaspoon salt
1 cup sourdough starter, at
   room temperature
3 cups unbleached flour
2 cups whole wheat flour

Using large bowl, pour hot water over margarine, stir to distribute margarine and cool water to 105 to 115 degrees. Then add yeast and pinch of sugar; let stand 10 minutes. Stir egg into sugar and salt and add to margarine mixture; add sourdough starter and the unbleached flour (3 cups); beat at medium speed with electric beater 4 minutes. Using spoon, gradually add whole wheat flour, stirring until dough rolls from side of bowl.

Turn dough onto lightly floured board; knead 10 minutes or until smooth and elastic. Grease bowl, return dough and roll it around to grease top. Lightly cover; let rise in warm place (85 degrees) about 2 hours, until double in bulk. Turn onto floured board again, very lightly knead for 30 seconds. Divide dough in half and use hands to press each piece in a 9-inch square. Shape by rolling as a jelly roll. Tuck ends under and place in greased 9-inch loaf pan. Shape second loaf.

Cover and let rise in warm place until double in bulk. Place in COLD oven. Bake at 400°F 15 minutes; reduce heat to 350°F and continue baking another 20 minutes. Remove from pans and cool. Makes 2 loaves.

Double this recipe and bake a second loaf for the freezer. Tightly wrapped it will keep fresh up to four months.

BANANA CARROT BREAD

1 cup mashed ripe bananas (2 to
   3 bananas)
1 cup sugar
¾ cup (1-½ sticks) margarine, softened
2 eggs
2 cups sifted flour

1 teaspoon baking soda
½ teaspoon each cinnamon and salt
1 cup finely grated raw carrot
½ cup chopped nuts — pecans
   and/or walnuts

Preheat oven to 350°F. In large bowl beat together banana, sugar, margarine and eggs, using electric beater. Beat 2 minutes at medium speed. Sift together flour, soda, cinnamon and salt, then fold into banana mixture. Stir in carrots and nuts. Spoon into greased and floured 9-inch loaf pan. Bake 55 to 60 minutes. Cool in pan 10 minutes; remove and cool on rack. Store overnight before cutting — or freezing. 1 loaf.

Vendors at Faneuil Marketplace in Boston feature these, served hot from their carts. They're no trick to make for parties, ball games and benefits. And don't forget the mustard!

SOFT PRETZELS

1 package active dry yeast	2 teaspoons sugar
1½ cups water (105 to 115 degrees)	1 teaspoon salt
4 cups flour	2 egg whites
	Kosher salt

Sprinkle yeast over warm water; add pinch of sugar and let stand 5 minutes. In large bowl combine flour, sugar, salt, then add yeast mixture and stir to blend. Turn dough onto lightly floured board and knead until smooth and elastic, about 10 minutes.

Cut dough into 18 pieces, then roll in floured hands to make strips about 14-inches long and ½-inch round. Twist these to shape pretzels and place on greased cookie sheets. Beat egg whites just to the frothy stage; brush over pretzels and sprinkle with the coarse salt. Bake in 400°F oven 15 minutes, until light brown. Serve warm or cold. 18 pretzels.

Take time to measure ingredients accurately (the night before, if you want to save time in the morning) then follow directions to the letter. Once the oven door is shut DON'T PEEK — the way to perfect popovers time after time after . . .

POPOVERS

1 cup unbleached flour	1 cup milk
¼ teaspoon salt	margarine
2 large or jumbo eggs	

Preheat oven to 375°F. Sift flour and salt into bowl; add eggs and milk and then beat with electric beater until smooth — 2 minutes. Grease muffin pans or custard cups with margarine; pour batter to half-fill containers. If using custard cups, place on cookie sheet or shallow baking pan for easy handling. Bake in oven 50 to 55 minutes. Serve hot. Makes 9 to 12 popovers, depending on size of baking cups.

YORKSHIRE PUDDING

Old-time favorite with roast beef: Popover batter is baked in cups containing a little of the fat and brown particles from the bottom of the roasting pan. When roast is about ready to leave the oven to "rest" before serving, raise the oven heat to 400°F. Grease baking cups generously with the hot fat and beef particles then half-fill with batter. Bake 40 minutes. Serve Yorkshire Pudding with slices of beef. Another time bake in shallow pan and cut Yorkshire Pudding in squares for serving.

Double this recipe, one to oven-bake and one to griddle-bake as Farls. Roll the soda bread dough 1-inch thick then cut in four Farls, which means quarters. Heat griddle or skillet hot over moderate heat and bake 10 to 15 minutes on each side. Check center for doneness. Farls are Scottish scones.

IRISH SODA BREAD

4 cups unbleached flour
½ cup sugar
1 teaspoon each salt and soda
2 teaspoons baking powder
1 cup raisins

1 large egg
2 tablespoons margarine
1½ cups buttermilk (or sweet milk with
   1½ tablespoons vinegar added)

In large bowl sift together flour, sugar, salt, soda and baking powder. Add raisins and stir. Fork-beat together egg and margarine to blend; stir into flour mixture. Stir in buttermilk just to make a moist dough — as for biscuits. Put on lightly floured board and knead with finger tips about 2 minutes, no longer.

Grease 9-inch layer pan and put dough in, flattening with fingers. Bake in 375 degree oven 40 minutes. Test center for doneness with cake tester. Serve warm. Delicious toasted. Makes 1 loaf.

Special treat: Serve the warm loaf with walnuts, to crack and dip into coarse salt. Pour chilled white wine; such as an Emerald Riesling.

Ruth Lenson bakes this Jewish Sabbath bread most Fridays, and always she says a prayer and places a little "bird" on the highest braid. "The bird will carry my thoughts heavenward, as my mother taught me," said the Massachusetts artist, writer and mother of three sons, who has taught breadmaking to so many.

CHALLAH

6 tablespoons margarine
1½ cups boiling water
2 tablespoons sugar
3 teaspoons salt
2 packages active dry yeast

½ cup warm (105 to 115
   degrees) water
¼ teaspoon sugar
3 eggs
7 cups unbleached flour

Place margarine in large mixing bowl; add boiling water, sugar, salt and cool to about 105 degrees (a drop on the inside of the wrist feels warm).

Meanwhile sprinkle yeast over ½ cup warm water and add a pinch of sugar for yeast to feed and grow on. Let stand 5 minutes, until foamy and full of bubbles.

Beat eggs, reserving 1 yolk for glazing top of loaves. Add eggs and the bubbly yeast to margarine mixture in bowl. Mix well and stir in 4 cups of the flour, then gradually add the remaining 3 cups flour. (Dough should pull away from bowl, add a little more flour — but only if necessary!)

Turn dough onto lightly floured board and knead until smooth and elastic, 8 to 10 minutes. Place dough in lightly greased mixing bowl, rolling dough to grease top. Cover lightly and let rise in warm place (85 degrees) until double in bulk. Takes about 1½ hours.

Punch down dough, divide into 3 parts.* Divide each into 3 more parts (now 9 in all). Roll each piece into a long rope and, using 3 pieces at a time, braid the pieces together into a loaf. Repeat to make 3 braided loaves.

Place each loaf in well-greased 9-inch loaf pan. Mix reserved egg yolk with 1 tablespoon water, dash of salt, and using pastry brush spread over the 3 loaves. Set aside to rise in a warm place 1 hour or until double in bulk. Bake in hot, 400°F oven 35 to 45 minutes, until loaves are a rich golden brown. Immediately take from pans and cool on wire racks. Makes 3 loaves.

*To make bird:

Before braiding loaves, pinch off piece of dough the size of a large walnut; roll between hands until it looks like string. Tie in a knot then pull and tuck one end to make the bird's head. A raisin for the eye, if you like. Place on loaf for the final rising.

Frozen Dough

When thawed overnight in the refrigerator, frozen dough makes a good loaf of bread, base for pizza, and it can be credited with the return of Fried Dough — breakfast or anytime treat that's deep fried, rolled in sugar and ENJOYED!

Frozen dough has yet one other possibility to save one portion of the big package to make Pidoni, bite-size goodies that originated in Sicily. Several of these make a good lunch or snack.

PIDONI

1 pound ground beef
1 large onion, chopped
1 green pepper, chopped
½ cup spaghetti or pizza sauce

salt, hot pepper sauce to taste
pizza dough
margarine

Cook ground beef in skillet over high heat until it begins to brown, add chopped onions and pepper, reduce heat to moderate and cook until vegetables are soft — not brown. Add pizza sauce and simmer 10 minutes, until thick. Taste for salt, add dash of hot pepper sauce. Take sauce off heat. Use rolling pin to roll pizza dough very thin; cut in 4-inch squares. Put a spoonful of filling on each dough square; fold to make triangle and seal edges by pressing with fork dipped in flour. Arrange pidoni on greased cookie sheets; cover lightly and let stand in warm place until dough is double in bulk. Brush tops with soft margarine. Bake in 400°F oven 10 to 15 minutes.

SPINACH FILLING

1 pound fresh or 10 ounce package
  frozen spinach
2 tablespoons margarine

1 large onion, chopped
½ teaspoon celery salt
1 cup cottage cheese

Cook fresh spinach in water that clings to leaves when rinsed under cold water or thaw frozen spinach. Both should be strained to remove extra liquid, then pressed dry with hands. Melt margarine in skillet and sauté chopped onion until soft; add spinach and celery salt. Mix well, taste for seasoning. Remove from heat. Place one spoonful of spinach atop 4-inch square pidoni dough (see recipe). Top with spoonful of cottage cheese and seal triangle. Let rise and bake as for pidoni recipe. 12 pidoni.

This basic recipe may be stored in refrigerator one week.

PIZZA SAUCE

2 tablespoons margarine
2 onions, chopped
1 green pepper, chopped
2 garlic cloves, minced
1 (32-ounce) can tomatoes

1 (6-ounce) can tomato paste
1 teaspoon each salt and sugar
1 teaspoon each oregano and basil
few drops hot pepper sauce

Melt margarine in 10-inch skillet; add onions, green pepper and garlic; cook over moderate heat until vegetables are soft, not brown. Add tomatoes and juice from can, tomato paste, salt, sugar, oregano, basil and hot pepper sauce. Heat to boiling; reduce heat and simmer, covered, 30 minutes. Makes 1 quart.

To make pizza:

Prebake pizza crust (see recipe) in 350°F oven 5 minutes; spread generously with this sauce then top with a wide variety: shredded mozzarella cheese, sliced mushrooms, strips of green pepper, onion rings, pepperoni, crumbled bacon, anchovies, sliced olives, cherry tomatoes etc. For a party, divide guests into groups and invite each of these to assemble their own pizza — as they choose. Bake near bottom of hot 425 degree oven 20 minutes, until pizza bubbles and begins to brown around the edges.

CHEESE FILLING

1 cup cottage cheese
1 cup Mozzarella cheese, cut fine
1 egg, slightly beaten
¼ cup finely chopped chives
   or parsley

1 teaspoon grated lemon rind
few drops hot pepper sauce

Combine all ingredients; taste for seasoning. Place one spoonful atop 4 inch square pizza dough, then fold and seal to make pidoni — ready to let dough rise to double in bulk before baking (see pidoni recipe).

Make lots and freeze for emergencies — a most delicious surprise! Hard-frozen these take only 15 minutes to bake in 350 degree oven. Serve bubbly hot.

BITE-A PIZZA

2 packages (12 each) refrigerated
   dinner rolls
1½ pounds bulk sausage, sweet or hot
1 (16 ounce) jar pizza sauce
1 (16 ounce) can plum tomatoes,
   drained and chopped

1 teaspoon each salt and vinegar
few drops of hot pepper sauce
1 garlic clove, minced
1 teaspoon dried oregano
1 pound sharp Cheddar cheese,
   shredded

Separate rolls into fourths; arrange on ungreased cookie sheets. Prick each several times with fork. Bake in 300 degree oven 10 minutes, until slightly browned.

Fry sausage in skillet until it crumbles and just begins to brown, while still moist remove from skillet and drain on paper. In saucepan heat pizza sauce, tomatoes, salt, sugar, hot sauce, garlic and oregano; simmer 10 minutes. Remove from heat and cool by setting pan over bowl of cold water.

On each biscuit piece, place a teaspoonful of sauce, another of sausage, then sprinkle with shredded cheese. Freeze until needed. OR bake at once in 375°F oven 10 minutes. Topping may be changed to include mushrooms, green and red peppers, olives, anchovies, etc. This recipe makes 96 small pizza pies for appetizers, snacks, impromptu suppers. Serve three of these with salad, cheese, fruit and glasses of Chianti or Zinfandel.

SESAME CRESCENTS

1 package (8-ounce) refrigerator
  crescent rolls
1 egg

1 teaspoon sesame seeds
1 teaspoon kosher salt

Open and spread out rolls, shaping them according to package directions. Beat egg with fork then use to brush rolls; sprinkle with sesame seeds and coarse salt then press with fingers. Bake in 375 degree oven 12 to 15 minutes. 8 rolls.

CHEESE BISCUITS WITH POPPY SEEDS

2 cups packaged biscuit mix
1 cup grated (¼-pound) sharp
  Cheddar cheese
2 tablespoons minced onion (instant
  if you like)

2 tablespoons poppy seeds
¾ cup milk

Preheat oven to 400°F. In bowl combine biscuit mix, cheese, onion and poppy seeds. Add milk at once and fork-stir to form a moist dough. Turn dough onto lightly floured board; knead lightly with finger tips, about 2 minutes. Pat dough ½-inch thick then cut in 2-inch rounds. Place in ungreased 9-inch square or round pan. Bake in oven 15 to 20 minutes, until biscuits are high and brown. Brush with margarine and more poppy seeds after baking if you like. Serve hot. Makes 10 to 12 biscuits.

SOUP OR SALAD STICKS

1 package refrigerator biscuits
milk
1½ cups rice cereal, coarsely
  crushed

2 tablespoons caraway seed, celery
  seed, dill seed or sesame seed
salt to taste
margarine

Preheat oven to 425°F. Cut biscuits in half; roll each part into pencil-thin sticks (about 4 inches long). Brush with milk. Mix cereal crumbs, seed and salt; roll sticks in mixture. Bake on lightly greased baking sheet for about 10 minutes, or until lightly browned. Makes 12 sticks.

Desserts

Dessert comes as the final course of the meal, and for many, the favorite. Derived from the French word, *desservir,* meaning "to clear the table," it can serve as the highlight of a celebration (Happy Birthday!), or as a pleasing conclusion to the meal.

Desserts can be anything from ice creams, puddings, cakes, pies and cookies to fruits and cheese. They are usually quite sweet, the theory being that sweetness dulls the appetite. But above all, they must be deserved — hence the expression "just dessert."

Many desserts can be fully or partially prepared and frozen. Here are some tips:

- The preferred method for freezing fruit pies is unbaked.
- Add extra gelatin to gelatin desserts to freeze as freezing has a tendency to cause separation.
- Pie or desserts with whipped cream topping should be first frozen, then wrapped.
- Pie shells may be placed on a large cardboard circle covered with plastic wrap. Separate pastry circles with plastic wrap. Overwrap with freezer wrap.

AMERICANA GINGER CAKE

½ cup (1 stick) margarine
½ cup sugar
1 egg
¾ cup unsulphured molasses
2 cups all purpose flour
2 teaspoons baking powder

1 teaspoon soda
½ teaspoon salt
1 teaspoon ground ginger
¾ cup buttermilk or plain
    yogurt

Topping

1 tablespoon melted margarine
3 tablespoons sugar
1 tablespoon flour

2 tablespoons grated orange peel
½ cup chopped nuts

Preheat oven to 350°F. Cream margarine with sugar, add egg, beat well. Stir in molasses. Sift together flour, baking powder, soda, salt and ginger. Add to creamed mixture alternately with buttermilk or yogurt. Pour into greased and floured 13 x 9 x 2 inch pan. Combine topping ingredients and sprinkle over batter. Bake 40 to 45 minutes. Serve hot with ice cream, whipped cream or warm applesauce.

MOLASSES MARBLE CAKE

2 cups sifted cake flour
1 teaspoon salt
2 teaspoons double-acting
    baking powder
½ cup (1 stick) margarine
1 cup sugar

1 teaspoon vanilla
2 eggs
⅔ cup milk
1 cup unsulphured molasses
1 teaspoon ground cinnamon
¼ teaspoon ground cloves

Preheat oven to 350°F. Sift together flour, salt and baking powder. Cream together margarine, sugar and vanilla. Beat in eggs. Add milk alternately with flour mixture. Beat ½ minute. Place ⅓ of batter in small bowl, stir in molasses and spices. Pour light and dark batters alternately into a well greased, lightly floured 8-inch tube pan or into a 9 x 9 x 2 inch pan. Gently run a spatula through batter to "marble." Bake tube cake 1 hour; bake 9 x 9 x 2 inch pan 45 minutes. Makes twelve servings. Serve plain or frosted as desired. Good cake to take to picnics.

½ cup (1 stick) margarine
1 (5-⅓ ounce) can evaporated milk
  ⅔ cup)
2 teaspoons salt
5 eggs
2 envelopes active dry yeast
1 teaspoon sugar
⅓ cup very warm water
1 tablespoon grated lemon peel

1 tablespoon grated orange peel
5-½ cups all purpose flour
*1 dry bean
1 cup confectioners' sugar
2 tablespoons water
vanilla or almond flavoring
candied citron slices
tiny candy decorettes
gold and silver dragees

Combine margarine, milk, sugar and salt in small saucepan. Heat slowly until margarine is melted, then cook to lukewarm. With a wire whisk in a large bowl beat 4 eggs; stir in milk mixture. Sprinkle yeast and 1 teaspoon sugar into warm water in cup (115°F) Stir to dissolve yeast. Let mixture rest until it bubbles, about 10 minutes. Add to egg mixture, blend well. Add lemon and orange peel. Beat in flour 1 cup at a time to make stiff dough.

Turn out onto a lightly floured pastry cloth or board; knead until smooth and elastic, turning dough occasionally. Add only enough extra flour to keep dough from sticking. Preheat oven to 375°F. Place in a large greased bowl; turn dough to coat all over with shortening. Cover with a towel. Let rise in a warm place, away from draft until double in size.

Temperature should be 85°F. Punch dough down when risen, knead a few times. Divide the dough in half. From each half make a rope-like roll about 20 inches long. Start coiling one in the center of a large cookie sheet, which has been greased with margarine. Keep the coil tight. Near the end, join the second half with your fingers, then continue to coil until all is used. Make the end of dough small so you can tuck it under easily.

Lift ring slightly and slip the dry bean into the dough near the center. Let the cake rise again in the same warm place covered with a towel. When dough has risen beat remaining egg in a bowl and brush the top of cake with egg. Bake in oven about 30 minutes, or until golden brown. It should give a hollow sound when tapped. Slide carefully to cooling rack. When cool frost and decorate.

Mix confectioners sugar with water in a bowl until smooth. Add vanilla or almond flavoring to taste. Drizzle over cake from a spoon tip until all is used. Decorate with candied citron, decorettes and dragees.

The person who gets the slice containing the *dried bean becomes KING or QUEEN for the day or the week.

This cake can be dressed up with ice cream or enjoyed with a sauce made from the plum syrup.

PLUM KUCHEN

2 cups all-purpose flour
2 tablespoons sugar
½ teaspoon salt
¼ teaspoon baking powder
½ cup (1 stick) margarine

1 (1 lb. 14 oz.) can purple plums
¾ cup sugar
1 teaspoon cinnamon
1 egg
1 cup dairy sour cream

Preheat oven to 375°F. Put flour, sugar, salt and baking powder in large bowl. Blend in margarine with pastry blender to make fine crumbs. Pour crumbs into 8-inch square glass baking dish; press firmly with fingers over bottom and halfway up sides of dish. Drain plums well, reserving juice. Cut plums in half and remove and discard seeds. Place cut side down over crumb-lined dish. Mix sugar and cinnamon; sprinkle over fruit. Slightly beat egg, then stir in sour cream thoroughly. Pour over fruit. Bake 30 to 35 minutes.

Sauce

Add 1 tablespoon cornstarch and ½ teaspoon almond flavoring to plum syrup. Cook over medium heat, stirring constantly, until sauce thickens. Cool before serving.

SKILLET DATE DESSERT

2 cups water
4 tablespoons margarine
2 cups brown sugar
2 cups all-purpose flour
½ teaspoon salt
¼ cup (½ stick) margarine

½ cup brown sugar
1 egg well beaten
¾ cup milk
½ teaspoon vanilla
1 cup dates, finely cut
½ cup heavy cream, whipped

Mix first three ingredients in a 10 inch skillet. Heat to boiling point. Simmer, Sift flour, baking powder and salt. Cream margarine and sugar. Add egg and beat well. Add dry ingredients alternately with milk. Add vanilla and dates. Drop pudding batter by tablespoonsful into hot sauce. Cover. Cook at a low temperature 25 to 30 minutes. (In an electric skillet, cook at 220°F.) Serve with sauce from the pan and garnish with whipped cream. 10 servings.

BROWN GOLD BARS

1½ cups all purpose flour
1½ teaspoons baking powder
½ teaspoon salt
½ cup (1 stick) margarine
⅔ cup brown sugar, firmly
  packed
1 egg
2 tablespoons grated orange
  peel, divided

¾ cup orange juice
2 teaspoons vanilla
1 (6-ounce) package semi-sweet
  chocolate pieces
1 cup confectioners' sugar
2 tablespoons orange juice

Preheat oven to 375°F. Sift flour, baking powder and salt onto wax paper. Set aside. Beat margarine and brown sugar until fluffy in a large bowl with electric mixer at medium speed. Beat in egg, 1 tablespoon orange peel, ¾ cup orange juice and vanilla until creamy and smooth. Stir in flour mixture with a wooden spoon until smooth; stir in chocolate pieces. Spread into a greased and floured 13 x 9 x 2 inch baking pan. Bake 30 minutes or until golden brown. Cool in pan or wire rack for 10 minutes. While cake cools combine confectioners' sugar, remaining 1 tablespoon orange peel, and 2 tablespoons orange juice in a small bowl until well blended. Drizzle over cake. Cool completely in pan. Cut into 48 bars.

An oven-baked dessert, this pudding makes its own sauce.

LEMON CAKE PUDDING

1 tablespoon grated lemon peel
½ cup lemon juice
1½ cups sugar
2 tablespoons margarine

½ cup flour
4 egg yolks
2 cups milk
4 egg whites

Preheat oven to 375°F. Grate lemon and extract juice. Cream margarine and flour in bowl; stir in lemon peel and juice; gradually add sugar to make smooth mixture. Beat together egg yolks and milk; stir into first mixture. Wash egg beater and rinse well; beat egg whites until stiff, but not dry. Lightly fold into yolk mixture, then pour into greased 2-quart dish; place in pan of hot water and bake 30 to 40 minutes. Press center of pudding with finger — it should feel firm. Serve warm from baking dish, spooning sauce from the bottom over cake-like top. 8 servings.

ELEGANT CHOCOLATE TRUFFLES

1 (6-oz) package semi-sweet
  chocolate pieces
1 cup orange juice
3 tablespoons light rum
1 (8½ oz) package chocolate wafer
  cookies, crushed

2 cups confectioners' sugar
1 cup very finely chopped walnuts
Chocolate decorating sprinkles

Melt chocolate pieces in top of double boiler over simmering water; remove from heat. Blend in orange juice and rum; stir in chocolate cookie crumbs, confectioners' sugar and nuts until well mixed. Cover; chill in refrigerator about 2 hours, or until mixture is stiff enough to handle.

Roll dough, a rounded teaspoonful at a time, into balls between palms of hands. Roll balls in chocolate sprinkles to coat generously, pressing firmly as you roll. Place on tray. Cover with aluminum foil; chill several hours or overnight. Store between layers of wax paper in metal tin with tight-fitting lid. Makes 6 dozen.

PEANUT BUTTER BARS

1 cup crunchy peanut butter
½ cup (1 stick) margarine, softened
1 teaspoon vanilla
2 cups brown sugar
3 eggs
1 cup all purpose flour

½ teaspoon salt
¼ cup confectioners' sugar
2 teaspoons water
¼ cup semi-sweet chocolate
  bits
1 teaspoon vegetable shortening

Preheat oven to 350°F. Put peanut butter, margarine and vanilla in large mixer bowl; beat at high speed until well-blended. Beat in sugar until fluffy; beat in eggs one at a time. Stir in flour and salt; spread batter in a greased 13 x 9 x 2-inch baking pan. Bake 35 minutes. Center should spring back when lightly touched with fingertip. Remove pan from oven to wire rack, cool slightly.

Combine confectioners sugar with water in small bowl; stir until smooth. Drizzle from a spoon over the cookies while still in pan. Swirl with bowl of spoon to make a sweeping pattern. Melt chocolate with shortening in a small bowl over simmering water. Drizzle chocolate from spoon over the white glaze, leaving open spots to make a black and white pattern. When cool, cut into 36 rectangles with a sharp knife. Carefully lift out of pan with spatula.

This is a make ahead party dessert to hold in the freezer. Choose ice cream holiday flavor: red peppermint for Christmas; pistachio green for St. Patrick and spring; ginger-pumpkin for Thanksgiving.

ICE CREAM PIE WITH COCONUT CRUST

2 tablespoons margarine
1 tablespoon milk
⅔ cup confectioners' sugar

1½ cups flaked coconut
1 quart ice cream

Preheat oven to 350°F. Heat margarine and milk until margarine is melted. Add sugar and coconut. Spread over bottom and sides of 9-inch pie pan. Bake in oven 5 minutes. Cool, then chill until firm. Fill pie shell with ice cream taken from freezer; freeze until firm, wrap and return to freezer until serving time.

CAPPUCCINO WAFERS

¾ cup all purpose flour
¼ teaspoon salt
⅔ cup sugar
½ cup (1 stick) margarine
2 tablespoons instant coffee
1 tablespoon dry cocoa (not mix)

1 teaspoon ground cinnamon
1 egg
½ teaspoon vanilla
cinnamon frosting
chocolate sprinkles

Preheat oven to 350°F. Sift flour and salt onto waxed paper; set aside. Cream sugar and margarine until fluffy in electric mixer large bowl at medium speed. Add coffee, cocoa and cinnamon; beat smooth. Beat in egg until well blended; beat in vanilla. Add dry ingredients a third at a time, beating just until blended. Drop by rounded teaspoonfuls two inches apart on greased cookie sheets. Bake 12 minutes or until edges are firm to touch and tops dry. Carefully remove from cookie sheets to wire racks; cool completely. Frost with Cinnamon Frosting; top with chocolate sprinkles before frosting sets.

Cinnamon Frosting

Beat 2 teaspoons water and ¼ teaspoon ground cinnamon into 1 cup confectioners' sugar until smooth. Use a small bowl with a wire whip. Makes about ¼ cup.

One of America's favorite flavors is mocha, that delicious blend of coffee, chocolate and dark brown sugar. Here's a cake that blends them delightfully.

COFFEE LAYER CAKE

½ cup (1 stick) margarine
1 cup brown sugar
2 egg yolks
½ cup unsulphured molasses
2 cups all purpose flour, sifted

½ teaspoon salt
3 teaspoons baking powder
½ cup cold coffee
2 egg whites

Preheat oven to 375°F. Cream margarine, add sugar gradually, continue creaming until mixture is light and fine grained. Add egg yolks. Beat until light and fluffy. Stir in molasses. Mix and sift the dry ingredients, adding ½ cup to the molasses mixture and the remainder alternately with the cold coffee. Fold in stiffly beaten egg whites. Bake in two greased 8 inch layer pans in moderate oven for about 25 minutes. When cool, fill and frost Fluffy Mocha Frosting.

Fluffy Mocha Frosting

½ cup (1 stick) margarine
4 cups confectioners' sugar
3½ tablespoons cocoa
¾ cup broken walnut meats

¼ teaspoon salt
⅓ cup (about) strong
   black coffee
1 teaspoon vanilla

Cream margarine. Combine sugar, cocoa and salt. Gradually add about half of sugar mixture to margarine, stirring to blend. Add remaining sugar mixture alternately with coffee until right consistency to spread. Beat smooth, add vanilla. Spread on cake and sprinkle with nuts.

ANGEL DRIFT ICE CREAM

3 tablespoons margarine
1 tablespoon milk
½ cup confectioners' sugar

1½ cups fine-grated coconut
assorted ice creams and sherbets

Angel Drift Shell:

Combine 3 tablespoons margarine with 1 tablespoon milk and heat just to melt margarine. Stir in ½ cup confectioners' sugar. Mix in 1½ cups fine-grated coconut. Spread mix in 9 inch pie pan. Chill well. Fill with scoops of different colored ice cream and sherbets to serve. Drift a cloud of flaked coconut over top.

VIENNESE MOCHA TORTE

2-½ cup all purpose flour
⅓ cup sugar
½ teaspoon salt

¾ cup (1-½ sticks) margarine
⅓ cup sherry wine
½ cup finely chopped walnuts

Preheat oven to 375°F. Mix dry ingredients in large bowl. Cut in margarine with pastry blender. When about size of dried peas, add wine gradually while tossing lightly with fork. Form into three equal balls. Turn three 8 inch layer cake pans upside down. Roll out 1 ball of dough on each ungreased pan bottom. Shape even with edge all around. Bake 10 to 12 minutes until lightly brown. Remove to cake rack to cool.

Filling

Stir 2 tablespoons dry instant coffee and ¼ cup confectioners' sugar into 1-½ cups heavy cream. Whip until spreading consistency.

Assemble

Put one cooled cake layer on serving plate. Gently spread with ⅓ of the whipped cream. Top with second layer cake; spread with another ⅓ of the cream. Top with third layer cake. Arrange remaining cream in bank around outer edge of top cake. Fill center with curls of semi-sweet chocolate. Sprinkle with additional walnuts. Chill several hours before serving.

Suggestion: cake layers can be made ahead and stored. If you like them soft as shortbread, store them with a slice of fresh bread overnight in a tightly closed container. Also, cakes can be made into 3 inch individual "cookies" instead of large layers.

HOLIDAY NUT BARS

½ cup flour
¼ teaspoon salt
1 tablespoon dry instant coffee
2 eggs

1 cup sifted light brown sugar
1 teaspoon vanilla
½ cup (1 stick) margarine, melted
1 cup chopped nuts

Preheat oven to 350°F. Grease 8 x 8 x 2 inch pan. Sift flour, salt and coffee. Beat eggs; beat in sugar and vanilla. Stir in flour, salt and coffee. Add margarine and nuts. Mix well. Spread in pan. Bake 25 to 30 minutes. Cut in bars, or squares, while warm. (For crisp bars, bake in 10 x 10 inch pan for about 12 to 15 minutes.) Makes 80 to 100 one inch bars.

DARCY'S IRANIAN COOKIES

½ cup firmly packed
   brown sugar
⅓ cup soft spread margarine
⅔ cup water
1 cup blanched almonds, ground
   (grind in blender)
1½ cups whole wheat flour

1½ cups quick-cooking
   rolled oats
1 teaspoon salt
½ cup chopped unblanched
   almonds
¼ cup sesame seeds

Preheat oven to 350°F. Combine brown sugar, margarine and water in a large bowl with a wooden spoon. Stir in ground almonds, then the whole wheat flour, oats and salt until well blended and smooth. Turn out onto lightly floured pastry cloth or board; knead five minutes, adding only enough extra flour to keep dough from sticking. Roll into rectangular shape 18 x 16 inches. Sprinkle chopped almonds and sesame seeds over dough; with rolling pin roll lightly into dough. Cut into 2-inch squares. Place on cookie sheets. Bake 10 minutes, or until cookies are golden; remove to wire racks with a spatula; cool completely. Store in container with tight-fitting lid. Makes 6 dozen.

FROSTED COFFEE BARS

1½ cups sifted all purpose flour
½ teaspoon baking powder
½ teaspoon soda
½ teaspoon salt
½ teaspoon (¼ cup) cinnamon
¼ cup (½ stick) margarine

1 cup brown sugar
1 egg
½ cup hot coffee (liquid)
½ cup raisins
¼ cup chopped nuts
coffee icing

Sift together flour, baking powder, soda, salt and cinnamon. Cream together margarine and sugar. Add egg and beat well. Add liquid coffee. Mix well. Add flour mixture to creamed mixture. Add raisins and nuts. Mix well. Spread in greased pan 12 x 8 inches. Bake 15 to 20 minutes at 350°F. While warm frost with coffee icing.

Coffee Icing:

Mix 1 tablespoon hot coffee with ½ cup confectioners' sugar. Add a drop or two of almond flavoring.

MOLASSES COCONUT CHEWS

2 cups sifted cake flour
¼ teaspoon soda
½ teaspoon salt
1 cup sugar
¼ teaspoon vanilla

1 cup molasses
⅓ cup margarine, melted
½ cup egg whites, unbeaten
1½ cup shredded coconut,
   packed lightly

Preheat oven to 350°F. Sift together flour, soda and salt. Combine sugar, vanilla, molasses and margarine. Quickly beat in egg whites. Add sifted dry ingredients all at once. Add coconut and stir to mix. (Do not overmix.) Line two 8 x 8 x 2 inch square pans with waxed paper; grease well with margarine. Pour batter into pans. Bake in oven 35 minutes. Immediately turn out on wire rack to cool. Remove paper. Cool about 5 minutes; turn right side up. When cold, cut each cake into 12 squares.

APPLE MERINGUE PIZZA

2 tablespoons lemon juice
3½ cups (about 4 medium) apples,
   pared, cored, and thinly sliced
1½ cups sifted flour
½ teaspoon salt

½ cup (1 stick) margarine
¼ cup quick-cooking rolled oats
4 to 5 tablespoons cold water
1 cup grated sharp Cheddar cheese
brown sugar meringue

Preheat oven to 425°F. Sprinkle lemon juice over apples. Sift flour with salt. Cut in margarine. Stir in rolled oats. Sprinkle with water, stirring with fork until dough is moist enough to hold together. Roll out on floured baking sheet to a 13 inch circle. (Baking sheet will not slip if placed on damp cloth.) Sprinkle cheese to within 1 inch of edge. Top with apples. Turn edge up over filling; cover with aluminum foil. Bake at 425°F for 20 minutes. Spread meringue over apples. Bake at 350°F for 18 to 20 minutes until meringue is browned. Serve as a snack or dessert, warm or cold. 8 servings.

Brown Sugar Meringue

¼ cup sugar
¼ cup brown sugar

½ teaspoon cinnamon
2 egg whites

Combine sugar, firmly packed brown sugar and cinnamon. Beat egg whites until slight mounds form. Gradually add sugar mixture, beating until meringue stands in stiff peaks.

Cobblers have been favorite fruit desserts from the beginning of American cookery. To "cobble" means to put together in a hurry.

PEAR COBBLER

3 cups fresh pears, peeled, cored
    and sliced
1 tablespoon lemon juice
⅔ cup sugar
1 tablespoon cornstarch

1 cup boiling water
1 tablespoon soft margarine
½ teaspoon ground cinnamon
Shortcake Dough

Preheat oven to 400°F. Peel, core and slice pears. Sprinkle with lemon juice to keep from browning. Set aside. Mix sugar and cornstarch in saucepan. Gradually stir in boiling water. Bring to boil; cook 1 minute stirring constantly. Then add sliced pears. Pour into 12 x 8 x 2 inch baking dish. Dot with margarine, sprinkle with cinnamon. Make up shortcake dough and drop by heaping teaspoonfuls on top of pears. Bake about 30 minutes. Serve warm with the juice and cream. 6 servings.

Shortcake Dough

1 cup sifted flour
1 tablespoon sugar
1½ teaspoons baking powder

½ teaspoon salt
3 tablespoons margarine
½ cup milk

Sift together flour, sugar, baking powder and salt. Cut in margarine with pastry blender. Stir in milk to make soft dough.

COFFEE-DATE BARS

1¼ cups all purpose flour
2 tablespoons instant coffee
    powder
1 teaspoon baking powder
¼ teaspoon salt

3 eggs
1 cup sugar
½ cup finely chopped
    pitted dates
½ cup coarsely chopped walnuts

Preheat oven to 350°F. Measure flour, instant coffee, baking powder and salt into a sifter. Beat eggs until light in large bowl with electric mixer on high speed. Beat in sugar slowly until thick. Sift flour mixture over and lightly stir in dates and walnuts. Spread in lightly greased 13 x 9 x 2 inch baking pan. Bake 35 minutes, or until a wooden pick inserted in center comes out clean. Cool in pan on wire rack; cut into 36 bars.

A favorite for beginners. Looks hard, but it is delicious and very easy to make. Serve warm or cold with ice cream.

APPLE AMBROSIA

6 cups (about 5) thinly sliced, pared, cored apples
⅓ cup orange juice
¼ cup (½ stick) margarine
½ cup light brown sugar

1 tablespoon grated orange peel
½ cup flaked coconut
½ cup all purpose flour
½ teaspoon ground cinnamon
1 quart vanilla ice cream

Preheat oven to 350°F. Put apples in greased 8 x 8 x 2 inch square dish. Pour orange juice over top. In bowl blend margarine and brown sugar well; add remaining ingredients except ice cream, and mix until crumbly. Spread evenly over apples. Bake 30 to 35 minutes or until apples are tender. 8 servings.

MEXICAN WEDDING CAKES

1 cup (2 sticks) margarine
¾ cup confectioners' sugar
2 cups all purpose flour

1 teaspoon vanilla
1 cup finely chopped pecans
confectioners' sugar

Preheat oven to 350°F. Beat margarine until fluffy in large bowl with electric mixer at high speed. Add the ¾ cup sugar, flour and vanilla. Mix well. Blend in pecans at medium speed.

Shape dough into 1-inch balls. Place 1-inch apart on cookie sheet. Bake 25 minutes, or until pale golden brown. Roll in confectioners' sugar while still hot. Cool on wire racks; roll in sugar again to coat evenly. Store in tightly covered tin with wax paper between layers. Makes about 3 dozen cookie-cakes.

PENNY WAFERS

2 tablespoons currants
1 tablespoon hot water
2 teaspoons rum extract
¼ cup (½ stick) margarine

¼ cup sugar
1 egg
⅓ cup all purpose flour

Preheat oven to 425°F. Combine currants, hot water and rum extract in small bowl; let stand about one hour to blend flavors. Beat margarine until soft in large bowl of electric mixer at high speed. Beat in sugar, then egg, beating until fluffy; stir in flour and currant mixture. Drop batter by teaspoonfuls, about 1½ inches apart on well greased cookie sheet. Bake 5 minutes, or until edges are golden. Remove from cookie sheet with spatula. Cool on wire cake racks. Makes about 2 dozen wafers.

BROWNIE PUDDING

1 cup flour
2 teaspoons baking powder
½ teaspoon salt
¾ cup sugar
3 tablespoons cocoa
½ cup milk

1 teaspoon vanilla
2 tablespoons margarine, melted
¾ cup brown sugar, packed
¼ cup cocoa
1¾ cups hot water

Preheat oven to 350°F. Sift into bowl, the flour, baking powder, salt, sugar and cocoa. Add milk, vanilla and melted margarine and mix until smooth. Pour into greased 8-inch square pan. Over top of batter sprinkle mixture of brown sugar and cocoa, then pour over top 1¾ cups hot water. Do not stir it in! Bake 45 minutes. Pudding forms its own chocolate sauce in bottom of pan. Cut in squares; invert on dessert plates ladling sauce over top. Serve warm, with scoop of ice cream if you like. 8 servings.

SWEET-SOUR LEMON SQUARES

½-cup (1 stick) margarine
¾ cup flour
2 eggs
1 cup brown sugar, packed
¾ cup shredded coconut
½ cup chopped walnuts and/or
   pecans

¼ teaspoon baking powder
½ teaspoon vanilla
1 teaspoon grated lemon peel
2 tablespoons lemon juice
⅔ cup confectioners' sugar, about

Preheat oven to 350°F. Crumble together margarine and flour, using fingers. Sprinkle evenly in 9-inch square pan. Bake in oven 10 minutes. Meanwhile, beat eggs; mix in brown sugar, coconut, walnuts, baking powder and vanilla. Spread over first mixture when taken from oven; bake 20 minutes longer. Mix lemon peel and juice with confectioners' sugar to make a thin frosting. Spread this over top as soon as pan comes from the oven. Cool. Makes 36 tiny pieces.

MARSH-MOCHA PUDDING CAKE

¼ cup sugar
¼ cup dry cocoa
1½ cups hot coffee
2 cups miniature marshmallows
1 cup all purpose flour
½ teaspoon salt

½ cup sugar
¾ cup sour cream
1 teaspoon vanilla
1 cup nuts, chopped
whipped cream or ice cream

Preheat oven to 325°F. Combine ¼ cup sugar with 2 tablespoons cocoa in bottom of 8 x 8 x 2 inch ovenproof glass dish. Add hot coffee; stir to dissolve. Sprinkle marshmallows over liquid. Sift dry ingredients and remaining 2 tablespoons cocoa together; add sour cream and vanilla and mix thoroughly. Stir in nuts. Spoon batter over mixture in pan stirring only to form a marbled mixture. Bake 40 to 45 minutes. Serve warm or cold topped with whipped cream or ice cream. 8 to 10 servings.

Easy to handle, just enough for one shell for 8 or 9-inch pie, or top crust for deep-dish pie.

PASTRY FOR PIE SHELL*

1 cup unsifted flour
¼ teaspoon salt

1 stick (½-cup) margarine
2 tablespoons coldest water

Combine flour and salt in mixing bowl. Add cold margarine cut in pieces. Then, using two knives or pastry blender, cut in margarine until mixture looks coarse — with some particles the size of peas. Sprinkle cold water, a tablespoon at a time over mixture. Use fork to toss and distribute water to make dough. It takes time to distribute water evenly, just to lightly wet the flour. Use hands to shape lightly into a somewhat flat ball. Wrap and chill while making filling — 2 hours or more if possible. Roll dough on lightly floured board; shape without stretching. Pastry for 9 — inch one crust pie.

***Double recipe for two-crust pie.**

A man's recipe; won $1,000 for "best flavor."

FIRST PRIZE APPLE PIE

8 large tart apples
pastry for 2 crust 9-inch pie
½ cup sugar
½ cup light brown sugar, packed
1 tablespoon flour

½ teaspoon nutmeg
grated peel of 1 lemon, 1 orange
2 tablespoons orange juice
½ stick (¼ cup) margarine

Preheat oven to 425°F. Pare apples, cut in quarters, core and slice thinly. Line 9-inch pie pan with pastry. Combine granulated sugar, brown sugar, flour and nutmeg; rub a little of this mixture into pastry. Add grated fruit peels to remaining sugar mixture. Arrange apples in pie pan, sprinkle each layer with some of the sugar mixture. Sprinkle with orange juice; dot with margarine. Cut remaining pastry in ½-inch wide strips; arrange as lattice over top of pie. Cut-off ends of pastry and crimp around edge of pie. Bake in 425 degree oven 40 to 45 minutes, until apples are tender. Serve warm or cold. 6 to 8 servings.

Such a pretty, tasty dessert it is hard to believe it is so low calorie.

DIETER'S DELIGHT PEACH PIE

Crumb Pie Crust:

1½ cups finely rolled zwieback
¼ cup sugar

½ cup melted margarine

Mix well. Line 9 inch pie pan with crumb mixture and pat firmly with fingertips or back of spoon. Chill until firm or bake 6 minutes at 375°F, and then chill.

Filling:

1 (3 ounce) package low calorie
    lemon-flavored gelatin
½ cup hot water
1 (8 ounce) can waterpack
    sliced peaches

½ cup orange juice concentrate
½ teaspoon almond flavoring
2 egg whites
¼ cup sugar

Dissolve gelatin in hot water and add juice drained from peaches. Add orange juice and almond flavoring. Chill until slightly thickened. Dice peaches. Beat egg whites, with sugar added a little at a time, until peaks form. Fold egg whites and peaches into gelatin mixture. Chill until it will hold some shape; then pour into chilled zwieback crust. Refrigerate until firm. 8 servings.

MOCK CHERRY PIE DIGBY COUNTY

3 cups fresh or frozen whole
    cranberries
½ cup seedless raisins
1¼ cups sugar
1½ tablespoons flour

½ cup hot water
grated rind of ½ lemon
pastry for 2-crust 8-inch pie
milk or cream

Preheat oven to 375°F. Toss together cranberries, raisins, sugar and flour. Mix ½ cup hot water and lemon rind then pour over cranberry mixture; stir. Pour filling into pastry-lined pie pan. Cover with top crust, trim and press edges, cut vents and brush with milk. Bake about 45 minutes, until filling bubbles through vents in top crust. Cool on wire rack before serving. One 8-inch pie.

TWO CRUST LEMON PIE

Pastry for 2 crust pie   2 lemons
3 eggs   1½ cups sugar

Make pastry from a mix or favorite recipe. Chill for 30 minutes, at least. Then divide dough in half; roll out one half and line an 8 inch pie pan. Keep remaining dough chilled. Grate peels from both lemons. Peel away all white pulp and cut lemons in sections as you do oranges or grapefruit. Discard seeds and connection tissues. Work over a bowl to catch all juice. Beat eggs slightly; beat sugar into eggs gradually. Now combine egg mixture with lemon peel, lemon sections and all the juice which has seeped out of the sections. Pour into unbaked pie shell, cover with top pastry; seal edges tightly. Bake 15 minutes at 425°F; then at 375°F. for 30 minutes or until crust is lightly brown. Makes a very thin pie with interesting sweet-sour flavor.

GEORGIA PEANUT PIE

To toast peanuts: remove from shell and place in shallow pan in 350 degree oven 10 minutes, until nuts are beginning to brown. Watch. Shake pan.

1 cup dark corn syrup   ½ teaspoon salt
3 eggs   1 cup whole toasted skinned peanuts
3 tablespoons flour   1 unbaked pastry shell (8-inch)
3 tablespoons melted margarine

In mixing bowl combine syrup, eggs, flour, margarine and salt. Beat with rotary beater one minute. Spread toasted peanuts in bottom of pastry shell. Pour filling over top. Bake in 350°F oven 30 minutes. Serve cold. 6 servings.

PARTY PUMPKIN PIE

1 cup canned pumpkin or   ¼ teaspoon ground nutmeg
  squash   ¼ teaspoon cinnamon
¼ cup light brown sugar   1 pint vanilla ice cream
Pinch salt   1 graham cracker pie shell
1 teaspoon ground ginger   ¼ cup chopped walnuts

Mix first six ingredients together in a large bowl. Soften vanilla ice cream and blend with the pumpkin mixture. Pour into graham cracker pie shell. Sprinkle with walnuts (or a crumb topping). Freeze two to three hours. 6 servings.

Index